1-800-FOR-SEALS-ONLY

contemporary writs by

CHRIS BENT
www.chrisbent.com

Published in the USA by
Chris Bent
Naples, Florida
USA

http://ChrisBent.com

1-800-I-AM-UNHAPPY,
1-800-FOR-WOMEN-ONLY,
1-800-LAUGHING-OUT-LOUD,
1-800-OH-MY-GOODNESS
1-800-FOR-SEALS-ONLY
and 1-800-BEST-FRIENDS-FOREVER
are trademarks owned by Chris Bent
and are used with his permission.

Cover Cammo Design courtesy of ███████████

————◆◆————

Also By Chris Bent

Available in Paperback and Electronic Versions

1-800-I-AM-UNHAPPY
Volume 1

1-800-I-AM-UNHAPPY
Volume 2

1-800-FOR-WOMEN-ONLY

1-800-LAUGHING-OUT-LOUD

1-800-OH-MY-GOODNESS

Coming Soon:

1-800-BEST-FRIENDS-FOREVER

DEDICATION

To Christina, Candice, Courtney, and their journeys . . .

IN THE WORDS OF OTHERS

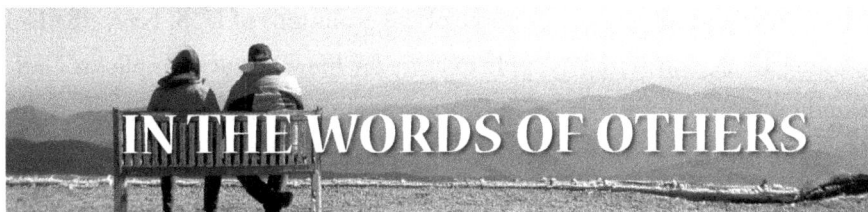

"Pungent, cogent, wistful, idealistic, naive, wise, — all in no particular sequence, reflecting a view of life that it is all unpredictable, and it is mental, physical & moral preparation that will sustain us… there are life lessons and observations here for anyone and everyone.…"

Lt (jg) James Hawes, BUDS 29E, SEAL, CIA,
(He was the First SEAL In Africa)…(sadly was my UDTR Instructor too)

Who knew SEALs could write? (LOL) But what Chris does with his gift is really less "writing" than it is expressing the "unwritten." We all have our thoughts; and Frogmen have certain very special and unique shared experiences. Chris puts the pen to the task of relating what we (the Frogs) have experienced and what we (all of his readers) now observe in sharing the experience of the world around us. It's challenging and funny (if you've been through a "real Hell Week"), and sometimes sad. But hey, isn't life? Hooyah!

Timothy Phillips, SEAL, BUDS 166, ST-8, ST-4

Chris - great stuff…as always. "Hooyah Mike"…"Every sin is a grenade"…"My wife is my swim buddy"…great thoughts as only a SEAL can put into words. I love it and will BUY a few copies for my Assistant Sergeant at Arms to read to guide their young lives… Hooyah Chris and see you soon

Phil King, Sergeant at Arms, NC Senate, BUDS 32

Mr. Bent's words of wisdom on some of the evolutions of U. S. Navy SEAL training are demonstrated to apply to everyday life with such simplicity. God, Family, Country, is the essence of being an honorable and patriotic American. It is the ethos of the Navy SEAL credo. The band of brothers whose lives are bonded as one in being; all for one and one for all! Nothing in this world feels better to receive in life as the emblem, the SEAL Trident, of a true warrior and to receive into one's heart the holy trinity! Hooyah! The only easy day was yesterday!

Erasmo Elijah Riojas (Doc Rio) HMC (SEAL) Ret.

I am a SEAL Teammate of LT. Chris Bent. During our years of serving our country as Naval Special Warfare Operatives, Chris always manifested that "Can Do" attitude so necessary for success in what many would consider: "A tough way to make a living!"

Among other sub-specialties, Chris and I had the honor of being the Platoon Commanders who would "Recover Astronauts!" Within the pages of "1-800-FOR-SEALS-ONLY", you will get to see the mind-set of students going through BUDS Training (still the toughest Military Training in the World) with most Classes experiencing an over 80% Drop Out Rate! Chris masterfully combines our training to current issues existing today. A Giant HOOYAH for a must read publication! 1-800-FOR-SEALS-ONLY is awarded a big BRAVO ZULU from your old Teammates!

Dr. Frank Cleary, OIC, Seventh Platoon, ST-2 (Ret.)

One need only look into the night sky to recognize that there is brilliance in chaos. One need only read this book to realize the same. Intertwined in stories, random thoughts, and opinions one will find extraordinary pearls of wisdom in here..........and a lot of them. Chris is brilliant.

Navy SEAL Commander

Dear Frogfather, Your writings remind me of the lessons and examples that were taught to me and my siblings by my parents, grandparents and the nuns that taught me in parochial school. I am so blessed to have them in my life. We are also blessed to have you because you have taken the time and effort to put down in writing your thoughts. They are insightful and positive to help us lead a better life. Thank you.

Maureen Murphy, Mother of LT. Michael Murphy,
Medal of Honor recipient, BUD/S Class 236, SDVT-1

Five Stars for the FROGFATHER!...This is a great book, and should be required reading....

Commander (SEAL) Tom Hawkins, USN, Ret., author, NSW Historian

Chris Bent has again taken his many and varied life experiences and applied them to life in general and "how to do it right". This book is clearly for everyone, not just SEAL's. Life was never meant to be easy and all of us can take away something from this book and the Frogman saying "The only easy day was yesterday". Even if it is the hard way....do the right thing.

From one Frogman to another I say to Chris, your eulogy (chapter 75) should be read when the time comes: Teammate, seen or unseen, you truly have made a difference! Hooyah 1-800-FOR-SEALS-ONLY!

Mike Macready, SEAL Team One, BUD/S 49 West Coast

Chris Bent's latest 1-800 offering certainly gets my SEAL of approval... Using his own unique blend of insight, intellect and inspiration, Chris lifts parallels from the rich history and tradition behind the US Navy SEALs to provide challenging questions and equally thought provoking answers to this experience that we call life. In this social-networking, politically-corrected day and age where common sense, discipline and values seem to have fallen by the wayside, Chris Bent cuts through like a K-Bar to remind us all exactly what is of the utmost importance.

Darren A. Greenwell - NSW Historian, Researcher, Collector.

"Chris is like a modern day prophet, throwing modern day concepts and concerns out there for us to contemplate. The seeds he tosses can land on sand or soil depending on the reader. I suggest you pull up a nice spot in your garden and sit down and read…then allow some of his thoughts to germinate in your life! "

Mia Guinan, Owner, Gourmet Gang, Camp Trident, Virginia Beach VA

"As a friend, Chris has helped me understand the inherent conflicts embedded in the language of 'political correctness' and how it attempts, and frequently succeeds, in disguising and defeating the 'truth.' Chris is engaged in a rhetorical battle — we need his insight."

William Lord, a 32-year-veteran Executive Producer and Vice-President of ABC News, and Professor of Journalism at Boston University

"Chris writes like he lives. As a man of distinction, he is a voice for the poor, a champion of the truth and a friend of strong character and conviction. His word and his service are a blessing to all who encounter him."

Vann R. Ellison, President/CEO, St. Matthew's House, Inc.

"Chris Bent is a very unusual person – Navy SEAL, Yale graduate, successful business owner, and radical Christian who is comfortable talking with anyone at any level in society. He doesn't just talk about faith or caring about the poor, Chris actually lives his faith and he works with the poor. His smile is genuine and reflects his deep joy in life, America, hard work, people and (most definitely) God. I have enjoyed reading his writings; they are different, often hard hitting and sometimes maybe even a little wild. Each one gives a fresh perspective on contemporary lives, reflecting Chris' intelligence and faith. Chris enjoys moving mountains."

Rev. Dr. Ted Sauter, Senior Pastor, North Naples Church

Prologue

This is meant to be a book for just one person. If just that one person is touched in some way to make their journey better, then the effort is not in vain. Each one of us can look back to one moment that changed our direction for the better. May this book, a collection of my writs and wit, find that pair of eyes.

Chris Bent

Kennebunkport
June 2015
www.ChrisBent.com

Contents

Chapters

*This is the 6th book in the 1-800 series to date. It includes
chapters from previous books and many new ones.
I dare you to put it down… LOL*

*I have had the humble honor to have been a member of the
Naval Special Warfare community. I was an officer in UDT-21, Underwater
Demolition Tteam 21. UDT-21 became Seal Team 4 two decades later.
From Hell Week to Apollo and Gemini recoveries it was quite a journey. Never
combat, but life has a way of challenging us all in other ways. I am humbled
before my brothers who have been the tip of the spear downrange.*

*How it all happened from a childhood fascination with the frogmen,
to diving, to the Navy, to being the first human to touch an Apollo spacecraft to
ever return from space, a small part of history, but nevertheless an honor.*

*Learning not to quit with wit and persistence and trust
and camaraderie was my blessing.*

*Using the language and images of that community I challenge
the reader to share my journey and to not quit. To not quit
on life, yourself, your country, and your God.*

Godspeed & hooyah mates.

1-800-FOR-SEALS-ONLY

inspirational writs by

CHRIS BENT

DDG 112 Hooyah

When something bad happens we all stop a moment and react.

Like when the earthquake was felt this week.

My wife and her girlfriends got scared and confused. Natural.

But when I talked with my buddies their immediate reaction was as mine… "What do I do right now?" "Who needs to be protected and how?" That is okay; that is the way life has been created. Nurture and protect; our primal roles.

Some things are meant to be natural, left alone… as they are part of nature, our nature. We are born. We die. This is natural. This is accepted. We can leave it alone or we can try to alter. Man can dignify it or man can desecrate it. Good or evil. Selflessness or selfishness.

Peoples' lives can pay tribute to life or they can cheapify it… (New word, cheapify, or cheapen… I like cheapify…) Hitler made life cheap. Our soldiers ennobled it. Love makes life beautiful. Addictions make life ugly.

When something bad happens something has to be done about it. "Done" does not mean debate! "Done" does not mean politicize. Nike

says "Just do it". So do I. Attack bad, don't dither it. Inaction is the very worst form of action.

We have a military because history has taught some of us that bad things have and do happen. Diplomacy works often but not always. There are people who lie no matter how much we give and try to understand.

We may even have to act without anyone else's permission. While all the public posturing is going on, there is not a day when someone in the military is not somewhere operating covertly, much less an innocent drone hovering for the next "perfect" kill. Our Special Operations and Intelligence communities have their lives on the line daily to allow us the delicacy of thinking peace is at hand, that we are safe. If something goes bad… our good guys are sent to situations you would cringe at, or withdraw into psychosis.

DDG 112 USS Michael Murphy was christened in Bath, Maine on May 7, 2011. I was honored to be there. I knew Mike at the start of his journey. Many of you may have read the book "Lone Survivor." Mike was a SEAL officer who was sent really deep into the bad. On a lonely mountain in Afghanistan he and two of his men were killed by the Taliban. One miraculously escaped and lives to tell the story. Mike took his final bullets standing with his radio so he could get clear transmission.

What one does for others is the measure of one's life. You can take bullets on a hill or you can take criticism in your home. It does not matter as long as you are standing up for good. Calling a spade a spade… calling bad for what it is, period.

We have become passive in our beliefs. We have become afraid to say out loud what we really feel, what our heart tells us. We don't listen to our heart because it may be politically incorrect. Proactive or passive about life? About values? About evil?

A year later in NYC, at the end of the commissioning ceremony on the Hudson River a yell by the 1,000 people there of "HOOYAH MIKE!" resonated in the piers and hearts nearby.

When I was told this, my stomach turned and my heart became heavy… and tears… because the word "Hooyah" is so unique to a very special community in Naval Special Warfare to which I once belonged.

Godspeed & Hooyah Mike.

Swim Buddy

Never get more than 6 feet apart.

BIG rule

BIG.

In the Navy SEALs, if you chose to ignore this rule, then on the next swim you would have a 4 inch 6 foot long hawser (rope) looped around your necks to keep you close together.

When you are swimming a mile or more in the ocean… and at night… and underwater…you need your swim buddy close so you can concentrate on your compass and navigating to your target. I preferred to keep my hand on my swim buddy's left hip, making sure he always knew where I was.

Swimming alone can be real dangerous. It was beat into our heads in our SEAL training. This is why I go nuts when I'm on a dive boat and everybody scatters once they are in the water. They have no clue. I do. SEALs do. Duuuhhh?

Marriage really demands the same respect. But we don't "get it" when we are young. And it is often too late when we are old. Hah! I bet you women want to really trust us and know where we are at all times. But,

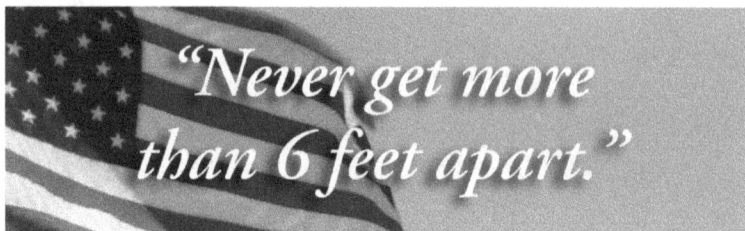

what if we want our independence and the thrill of a little flirt once in a while?

We should be going to church together. We should always take our kids to things together. Kids should know togetherness. They should feel you are their swim buddy too. Trust.

My wife drives me nuts wanting to know where I am every minute. Maybe that is the way it is supposed to be?

Maybe what they taught us in the Navy is really more profound. All of it was about trust. Going into foreign places where danger exists requires a lot of training, and trust...deep trust.

We all have our friends we think we trust. Some we have known a long time. Some talk behind our backs. You don't know who you can really trust until there is a real test.

One has to care more for the other person than self. You know it when it exists. The hawser teaches trust. It keeps you close.

Life is one big swim through all kinds of eddies and turbulent currents, even enormous waves that capsize you. When you have been sucked to the depths and come up coughing water and gasping for a breath, your swim buddy is at your side. Then you know trust. Maybe even love.

Kick, stroke, check your compass, check your depth. That hand is on your hip. That marriage is there for the kids and…. Yourself. That is real living, real family. All else is a delusion.

Ultimately, partners die or leave.

There is one swim buddy you can always count on.

You can read about Him in the New Testament.

Hooyah.

The Hard Way

"Mom, I won't do it.

"Leave me alone."

"You don't understand me."

Squirming to hide their arrogance and insecurity, the child, then the teen, then the 20-something basks in their new-found independence. Independence from rules, values, and you. It has become the "Mom, Whatever!" generation. The new demographic.

The Truth of the matter is that Moms really do know you better than you know yourself 90% of the time. Powerful statistics that have existed since the beginnings of man.

My way is my highway.

Every person is sent down their self-made highways of circumstance. In Western civilizations at least. Forget it in those other cultures. There, "Mom, Whatever!" might mean capital punishment… like death or at least cutting off part of your body or being sold.

Why have we always chosen the "me" path?

When you are young and healthy you feel so in control.

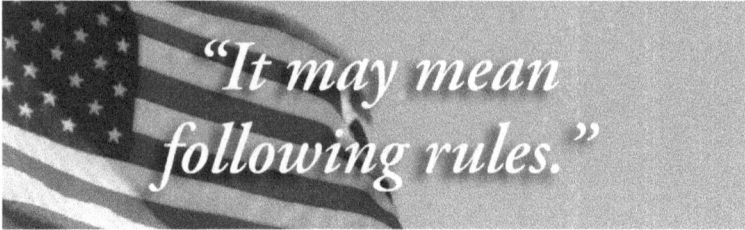

With indestructible bodies that flaunt regulation. This is the easy path. Your peers lead you down it with innocence and ignorance. Party. Go to work. Party. Unless you are poor.

There is now the keyboard culture with their ear buds comforting the insecure mind. Keyboard fantasy. Life is centered in the keyboard. Makes it easy to avoid responsibility. Avoiding responsibility is easy, just do it.

But if one ever chooses to look up, you will find people engaged and making a difference. They have chosen the hard way, for whatever reason. The hard way is learning from others, listening, avoiding mistakes, and learning from them.

It may mean following rules. It may mean showing others respect. It may mean getting the word "me" out of your vocabulary. It may mean showing your parents respect regardless of their flaws.

I know someone who never felt wanted. Her parents left her alone. Yet she forgave, and cares for her father to this day. He doesn't deserve it. Or does he?

The hard way is to become a nobody to yourself, and become a somebody to someone else.

The hard way is to follow your conscience, not ignore it.

Therein lays your Truth and the code to making the hard way the easy way.

Your choice.

The SEAL's choice.

Hooyah.

The Grenade

Mike Monsoor was Navy SEAL.

Mike won the Congressional Medal of Honor.

Mike is dead.

You see… He, fellow Seals, and Iraqi soldiers they were working with were on a rooftop on September 29, 2006 in Ramadi. A live grenade appeared. All would be killed or injured. Mike reached deep inside where Truth lives and dove on the grenade. His defining choice.

God bless you Mike.

Teammates were saved.

They hammered their Tridents onto his coffin.

Most of us are never asked to make that kind of decision. Really? I am not so sure. Mike defined choice. He defined what serving is. He chose to serve his buddies with his life. He said, "There is black and there is white." He said, "There is evil and there is good."

You want to debate??? Then go in the corner and hang an idiot sign around your neck. I'll bring you some animal crackers in an hour.

"They hammered their Tridents onto his coffin."

OK, I feel better. But this is all too important to dismiss quickly. Mike became THE role model of role models in that instant. The same can be said of Michael Murphy and unseen others…

Every moment of every day something bad happens. Every bad thing is witnessed by someone. Every bad event is initiated by some bad choice. A person is responsible for that choice. Think about it. People make evil possible. A grenade is a really big bad thing. But… what about the small grenades of life? Does a lie ever have the potential to cause great harm? Does a lie actually damage the liar, much less the person who is lied about?

As we all know there are a bunch of sins I could list and there are the famous Commandments I could refer to in helping to define things that cause harm.

And… How about a simple swear word that begins with an "F" uttered in earshot of a young child? The first time that word would ever be heard. Is there any way to know what seed may be planted…of an innocence lost? Would you want that responsibility? Was this not a potential grenade to this young life? Maybe???

Who is to know? In fact every wrong thing we witness in the course of a day is a potential grenade to someone. Maybe we should look at life through Mike's eyes and react with Holy instinct and attack? Or do we out of habit and political correctness look away and busy ourselves with something else... Some work task that is more important? Or maybe turn up the volume of our headphones and sing "Chasing Pavements" along with Adele...???

I want us to give Mike the Medal of Value. That medal can only be created and given to him by our actions. "Here Mike. I did this because of you. Your example made me do it."

I want to be true to my inner core and see more mini-grenades in the course of each day and right them. Stop them in their tracks. To tell the person who perpetrates that they are doing wrong. I want to do it out loud so others hear.

Too bad if feelings are hurt. Too bad.

Take the criticism and be proud.

It matters.

Be humble.

Every sin is a grenade.

Do something about it.

Thank you Mike.

Hooyah.

The Trident

The Trident is a symbol of three things.

No I am not talking about the Trinity, not today.

Do good things come in threes?

Wonder what else comes in threes???

How do we survive without threes?

How do we just survive? How do we make something out of nothing? Does a child come from nothing? What keeps us from becoming nothing? What happens when we sit around and do nothing? Nothing. Nothing at all. Maybe I should have entitled this piece "Nothing."

If I want to get a driver's license and don't study, what happens??? Nothing. If I don't go to school, what happens??? Nothing. If I don't put any effort into my life what happens? Nothing again. One's life becomes defined by self-inflicted nothingness.

The opposite extreme of this is the pursuit of a thing called the Navy SEAL Trident. Being mega-proficient in three elements… Sea, Air, Land.

Exhausting, brutal, cold, preposterous conditions for months on end. Sleep deprived… running endlessly in sand, swimming endlessly in the

> ## "No knowledge is the devil of accomplishment."

cold ocean, and ultimately dropping in exhaustion in the night with your wits intact. In and out of any element at any time. Mastery of weapon, mind, and body so challenging that 90% give up. Kind of like life when so many give up on their dreams or values or self.

There is not a day that goes by that you do not read about a tragedy where someone quit. To quit means that to try no longer has value. But if you don't try to do something how do you learn or grow? When they put my first bike in front of me it was scary. Had I not said "no" to fear I never would have known the wonder of a 10-speed or a motorcycle. Had I said no, I would have had no idea of what I was going to miss. No knowledge is the devil of accomplishment.

Today it is as hard finding employees as it is finding employment. Conundrum. Stupid. Hard work brings dignity and sense of self-worth. Blame the worker who underperforms. Blame the company who over-structures and loses the human touch. Profit without ethics is unseen terrorism. Administrative shields have dehumanized communication. We are reaching the sophisticated day when a call to Human Resources is answered by voice prompts… Just wait….

The old fashioned notion of teamwork has been destroyed. Oh, yes, there are teams in corporations with assignments… but for the most part they are jokes.

When I talk Team I know what I am talking about. In fact, look at the world of sports. Team sports. It is amazing what the champions achieve against all odds with an improbable mix of characters. Something intangible happens and they play like a pure team, being able to communicate without words. Analog, not digital. Capiche?

Same can be said for many small businesses as their team is so tight that they don't need the overhead of excessive administrative activities. Yet with the computerization of all aspects of business today there is no longer a useful team environment where humans feel bonded in task execution. And… the terrain becomes really fertile to quitting and moving on… and quitting and moving on…

This exploration of a quitting-minded culture could be characterized as a moment in history where a society undercut its glory and failed. A time where efficiencies of human interaction were dismissed to a balance sheet. A time where we quit on human.

On a SEAL Team no one has quit who is there. No one will quit regardless of the danger assigned. Being human has returned to basic values and they are worth dying for… the old values that were the foundation of our freedom and our pleasure.

Quit on God and you have nothing…

Hooyah.

57 Virgins

Why do men want so much?

Back in the beginnings of civilization or even existence, the male of our species was the provider and protector.

He was in charge of life and death, rules and punishment.

The woman was in charge of birth, nurturing and pleasure.

Over the millenniums more and more rules were established to protect order and fragile justice. Life was tribal. Then cultures formed creating new interpretations of old rules.

Not all that much fine print on scrolls? Men fought the wars. Killed off enough to rule for a while until the cycle repeated itself. Woman was always second and mainly voiceless. Pleasure for the male was insured by laws…harsh laws… which still stand in significant parts of the world today. Look at the headlines.

Women's rights are still at a standstill in Africa, the Middle East, and the Orient… It ain't right. Meanwhile we dither about our glass ceilings…

I don't need to be promised 57 virgins to go to heaven. That is sexist too. I don't dream about flopping around naked on clouds in exotic heavenly pleasures.

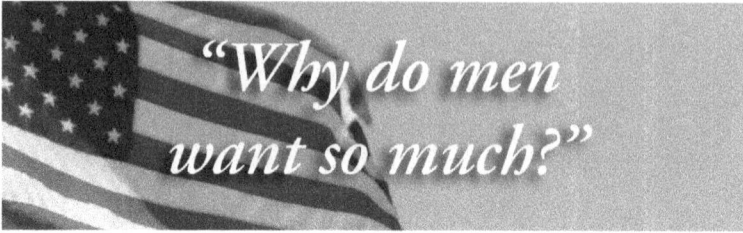

"Why do men want so much?"

Anyone who promises such is lying. I just want the assurance I get to see my Mom and Dad again... and get to know their parents, and their parents' parents. I believe I cannot kill anyone if I want to get there. I believe I have to ask for forgiveness to qualify. I want to be able to receive forgiveness from all who I had hurt. It may take a little time... but that would be heaven to me.

Rules should be made for human beings, not genders.

They should all be updated and simplified so they can easily be texted and shared on Facebook. Get governments out of the rule business. It seems like they are adding amendments and qualifications weekly. Who can keep track of all the fine print? Sign here??... and be held accountable in cyber-space for eternity.

Oops... I didn't read the fine print.

It is only two old virgins.

Hooyah.

Free Ascent

Did you ever think of an elevator as a free ascent?

What are elevator shoes? LOL.

To divers a free ascent means you are down deep and only have the breath in your lungs to rise to the surface and safety.

To the surface where you can breathe again. Hopefully unassisted.

You can free ascent from 12 feet and you can from 100 feet, if… you know what you are doing.

But if you hold your breath too tight, the air in your lungs will expand.

If you don't relieve the pressure and let bubbles come from your mouth evenly you will burst your lungs.

And if you let all out too soon you just might sink and "it's all over folks".

You might have to leave your dive gear on the bottom or just ditch it if you are in any danger. Like we trained from a diving bell and then a submarine.

Have to have a little confidence to pull it off.

One gets confidence from training and Trust.

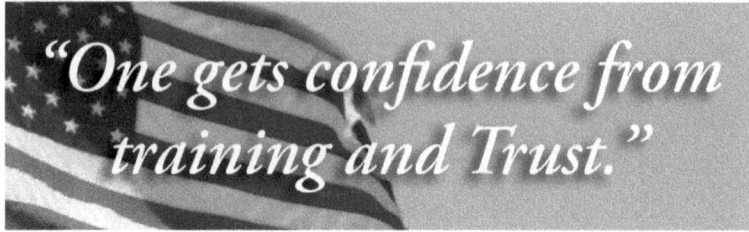

"One gets confidence from training and Trust."

People get in over their heads in life and get to places that are hard to get out of too. Physically, financially, emotionally, and spiritually.

Often the only way out is up and you have to ditch all your bad habits and self-centered preconceived notions and start over. From scratch. From nada.

The way is up. A free ascent. Not knowing where the surface is. Where does one get the Trust to let go and hold one's breath properly?

Look Above first.

Then gently kick your feet towards the sky and the Light.

No charge.

Free Ascent.

Hooyah.

CO2

I have a friend, Philippe, who believes that CO_2 is our number one priority.

Global warming and carbon dioxide are apparently the number one enemies of the moment. Hmm…

When I was a kid, you know… mid 20's… the Navy taught to me swim at night by using the Emerson Closed Circuit Rebreather. It gave off no bubbles so no one knew you were swimming under their ship to attach a limpet mine that would go off long after you had swum away. There was this chemical called baralyme, a mixture of calcium and barium that acted as a CO_2 absorbent in a filter that was part of the breathing path. The problem was that if water leaked in then the baralyme would not absorb the CO_2 which was toxic. Then you would rebreathe it and die.

So we did not like CO_2. We liked living. Well, our planet does not like excessive CO_2 and we should be finding ways to filter and reduce it. Let's have the North and South poles happy again.

At the same time I wish all this CO_2 fervor could be channeled into all kinds of other issues like cruelty to humans. We have the SPCA. Where is the SPCH?

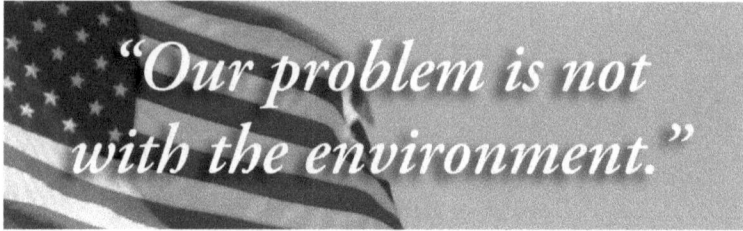

"*Our problem is not with the environment.*"

Where do these politicians and leaders (choke) in all these other countries have the gall to watch their own poor suffer and die while they are having great meals every night???

Shame also on the many that treat women like animals.

Where is the SPCW?

Why are we and all our media not crying out in rage at these even more pressing tragedies? Why do we ignore the torture and abject denial of human rights and dignity in North Korea, much less the Middle East… and all the other places that are protected by political correctness?

Why?

Is CO_2 poisoning already creeping into our bodies??? Why is our judgment so impaired? What has happened to our values??? We don't have to bomb… but where is our outrage? Why are we always apologizing?

Come on America!

Do you believe in anything? Do we just withdraw from the truth until the next major war? How come our veterans and servicemen are so patriotic? What do they see that we don't? Why are they silent when they return…? Is it because they don't think we can understand? Or care???

They know values. Do we? Values are the cornerstone of our democratic society. They have been forged in blood and sacrifice for centuries. And now we act as if they were archaic principles not that relevant to our digital age. That our Judeo-Christian Constitution is old parchment riddled with holes and outdated irrelevancies.

Our problem is not with the environment, it is with us. We individuals do not make our individual stands. We are asking government to take responsibility for all our needs rather than forging them out of collective individualism.

Each of us squanders. Each of us is responsible. My Dad always said, "Turn out the lights Chris." I do to this day. But we could watch all that we do. Use less energy. Become energy efficient. Become values efficient.

We need to manage our own details.

We don't look as healthy as we used to. We have legislated so much out of what should be normal. Where are the afternoon athletics in schools? Where are the values that used to be taught in schools?

Let's take the blame ourselves in a courageous act of accountability.

The endangered is man.

We are the pollutant.

God help us.

Hooyah.

Boundaries

Boundaries are made to help us know which is our land and which is someone else's.

There is usually a fence along the boundary of the property which clearly shows all where your land is.

Out west there is barbed wire, on borders tall fences.

Sometimes boundaries are rivers or oceans.

Countries are so defined.

Then again in some wildernesses or deserts there are no fences and the boundary is not visible. Now you don't want to cross over the border boundaries of some countries like North Korea or Iran for fear you might just go right to jail. Pain included.

In another sense, age can be a boundary or a limit to what one can do. Intelligence can be a boundary, as ignorance can limit one's journey. Race can be a boundary, as it limited movement in our past. Religion sets all kinds of limits that people can either follow or ignore. Much to talk about.

Regardless, boundaries define much of all we can do. If we choose to

ignore them then someone will charge us with trespassing and criminal behavior. If we don't have the better lawyer we can end up in a small room with bars on the window and crummy food... and even torture...

So boundaries are important. Yes???

But then nobody, much less young people, wants someone else telling him what to do or where not to go.

So who respects boundaries these days???

There certainly are no moral boundaries anymore. All you have to do is click the box saying you are over 18 and there are no boundaries.
Or uncheck the box Parental Supervision Recommended and whoosh... all boundaries disappear and your fantasies are in high definition.

What about language? There are so many new words that are not yet in the dictionary that we can talk without boundaries or respect for others, much less ourselves.

Now we ask and allow our government to redefine our boundaries all the time. They love to do it. The politics of legislation. Moreover, we want them to do it! Then blame can be meted out to all those who do not respect the regulations, laws, and ordinances. We don't have to worry about what is right or wrong. It is already codified or written into law.

However, with so many laws it is no longer easy to discern boundaries. We need lawyers to help us. Fine print protects all but us. Voice prompts keep us from crossing communication boundaries. Where are we?

I have come across a fantastic family where all they know is boundaries and discipline. Where "NO" was the operative word, not "Yes."

Work ethic, respect, quality behavior, abnormal intelligence, and logic abound in their sons. Punishment was the reward for trespass.

This family has their next generation prepared for reality not fantasy. To me they are the new American model.

Boundaries are great.

The Right ones.

If we wish to be great again we might try to get back to those oldest 10 boundaries…

They are in the No.1 best-selling Book of all times.

Click and you can download it.

Hooyah.

The Drill Instructor

The Drill Instructor (DI) barks out his commands to the frightened cadre.

"Gimme 50!!!"

"Backs straight!!!"

"Chest must touch ground!!!"

"Full extension!!!"

"Get that back straight!!!"

"How many times do I have to tell you?!!!"

"OK, stay at lean and rest until I come back, children!"

Do you think they make Marines, soldiers, much less SEALs by asking them what they would prefer to do? Do you think the Drill Instructors have graduated from sensitivity training? Are Democratic Constitutional rights in effect? Are the recruits entitled?

I postulate that this just might be about life and death, not feelings. I think this may be about protecting your freedoms and right to complain. But this cannot happen without young men prepared for battle and for death.

"You have got to be kidding!"

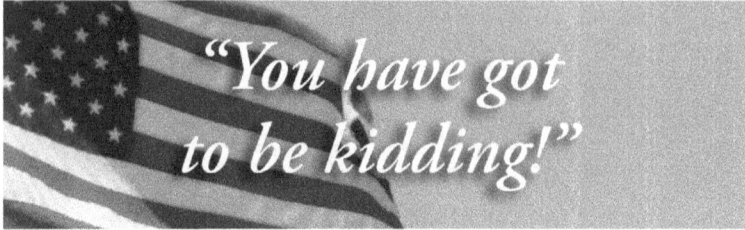

Huuuhhh??? Hello?? You have got to be kidding! OMG you can't be serious! Death doesn't happen other than on the news and usually far away. Whatever. Text me later…I am busy.

I am of the opinion that every young able-bodied male should be drafted. Boys become men much sooner than on the playing fields or the streets.

We sure don't like systems which tell us what to do. It is like it is in our DNA to rebel against authority. Go away Dad, go away teacher, go away policeman, go away boss, go away reality. I am armored with my self-serving iPhone and the courage of my social network.

We allow the Drill Instructors of life to make us miserable as long as it keeps us from getting killed. We love our bodies as they are our ego cathedrals.

But what about the Drill Instructor in the clouds? He wants to save our souls and enrich our lives beyond our wildest imagination. Problem is… we don't have any imagination.

How many individuals choose paths right into the combat zones of greed, lust, envy, pride, gluttony, anger, and filth? Drugs, alcohol, sex, vanity, indifference, and jealousy and… on and on. "Well, I didn't think it would be this bad. A little more won't hurt…" Consciences trampled by disdain for authority and distain for logic.

Where is the Drill Instructor when I need him? Everyone doesn't screw up their lives. I see some happy people around… No, not the hypocrites… just a lot of normal people going about their business, helping others, and laughing. How do I become one of them?

Well, duuuhhh???

Hello, The Drill Instructor in the sky!

No pain no gain they always said…

Hooyah.

Escape Trunk

One of the coolest things in the world for a diver is a place called the Escape Trunk.

Harry Houdini probably invented it. Wait… Which came first? Houdini or the Submarine?

You Google it. I am not.

In any case it is so exciting and so simple.

Second only to today's Navy SEALS doing ocean free fall with all their gear on is the SDV and escape trunks.

An escape trunk is a small cylindrical chamber with hatches on the top and bottom into which can squeeze 2 divers with Scuba, O2, or mixed gas… In all submarines so men can escape from the submarine. Climb a ladder from within up into the escape trunk. Close the bottom hatch. Flood the thing fully with seawater. Equalize. Then open the top hatch and swim out onto the deck of the submerged submarine. You are 30-60 feet down. All your men repeat same then collect on the Conning Tower before peeling off on a mission. At night the phosphors in the Caribbean were spectacular coming off the bow. Magical and mystical.

All should have such experiences…. But to do so takes a bit of training and never quitting. No pain no gain they say…

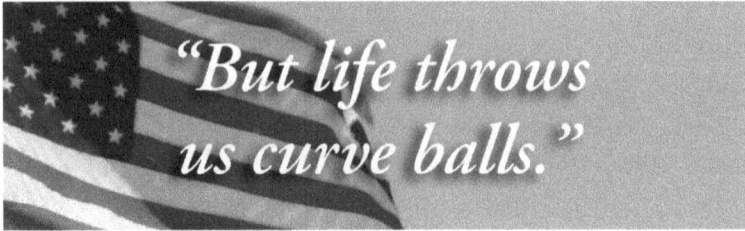
"But life throws us curve balls."

But life throws us curve balls. We get into situations we choose that are hard to get out of. Really hard. Be it economic or medical or moral we find ourselves in uncomfortable places. Marriage and family get complicated.

The easy out does not exist, though in a self-centered arrogance we think we can. Look at the downward spiral of the addict. How difficult it is to find an escape trunk.

Taking a first step and not quitting is the only path up.

This applies to everything in life.

Admitting error and asking for forgiveness.

The irony of all this is that the way out is only up.

If we all looked up instead of down we might find the path that has always been waiting for us.

Don't quit.

Some call it the Divine path.

Hooyah.

War

"War is an ugly thing, but not the ugliest of things. The decayed and degraded state of moral and patriotic feeling which thinks that nothing is worth war is much worse…" (John Stuart Mill).

I have never used a quote before… but I just finished an intense book by a SEAL, "Damn Few." This jumped out at me so strong as it is themed throughout all my writs. So let's explore it a little… And see if we can reject the premise.

As we all know war is repugnant because of all the innocent people that suffer horribly from wounds and displacement, much less death. Idiotic regimes, egos, and cultures espouse freedom and compassion for their poor only to subjugate them to false cultures of corruption. While, at the same time, demonizing our liberties and success. With our great intellects we dismiss their posturing as just illusions of danger.

We analyze and yield responsibility to the talking heads and pundits in the media. They are all about their perspective, their truth, and the infinite postulations of politicians. They are more right than we are? We allow them to be… and we become complicit in the advent of war.

I have never seen a body blown to bits or a child with a bullet hole in her head. Do I need to see that to take a stand? Do I need to turn off

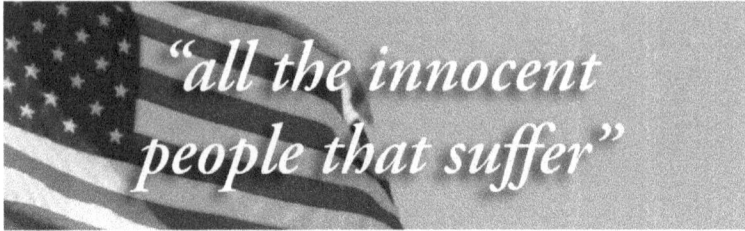

the TV and do something? Can I stop a bullet coming for some child's brain?

We all have to answer that question. We all have to think about it and take a stand. Not to take a stand is to be a coward and an irresponsible adult who chooses to facilitate evil. That's how I call it.

To take a stand means to stand for something. Where is the line you draw? Does anything have value? Define values. Whatever made this country great? Or when did you think it might have been great?

We are a good people. We are a blessed people. We have a great Constitution and a great history of compassion. Is this worth protecting? Do we realize we are on an invisible slippery slope to losing it all?

There is a moral decay in our country that is almost systemic. Laws are reducing responsibility. Behavior is being redefined to permit anything under the umbrella of rights. Sin now has rights. Christians are now being marginalized. Showing the flag is now problematic. Labels have proliferated such that anything good is easily categorized as bad. It is so subtle. It is so deadly.

Our internal bickering and blaming is eroding our society. The rest of the world sees it as weakness and the forces of war are being emboldened.

We will be at war again. It may be this year… or next… but it is inevitable the way we are behaving.

"Nothing is worth war" is becoming our motto.

We are actually saying that we will not fight.

We will talk and threaten while our economy and our military erode.

Paper tiger.

Our children aren't worth war?

If you touch my car I will kill you.

Hooyah.

No AC

No AC.

You mean no air conditioning??

OMG, what are we going to do?

I am not going to work.

I'll go sit in the car until you get it fixed!

Yes, summers in St. Louis, Philadelphia, and New York City get mighty hot. Sweltering. Steam on the pavements hot. All one can think of is the beach or autumn. In fact you beg for deep snow... kinda...

One can travel to Egypt. One can travel to the Vatican. One can travel to Moscow, London, Paris, Mexico City, or Jerusalem... and find amazing structures, amazing buildings, and more than amazing churches.

Oops, they had no computers, no typewriters, no phones, no trucks. Yet they built and built in unimaginable testimony to the potential of man. Today they are being bombed to rubble in wars far away. Evil hates accomplishment.

How did they do it? The Duomo in Milan with her handset arches

"You mean no air conditioning??"

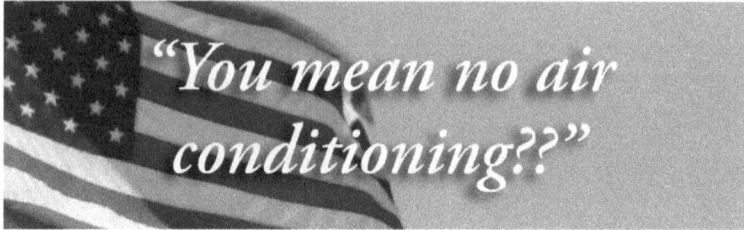

with her unique precision stones is just art. Hey, no power tools or forklifts.... Amazing.... Today we have so many committees and building codes that no grandeur would have been possible.

Man worked like an ant to raise his imagination toward the heavens. Pyramids.

But most disturbing and logic defying of them all was it was done with No AC! No Poland Spring bottled water. No sanitizer. No paper towels. No aspirin.

But no air conditioning???!!! They had to be crazy. Insane crazy.

But maybe, they just had no choice. Maybe they had no clue of what was better. Maybe not knowing is better than knowing....

They did great in spite of no AC, go figure.

Today is a very dangerous time. Evil abounds, unless your head is in some ideological sand. We don't want to sweat. We want machines and computers to do things for us. Oh, just send in the SEALs. They will do our sweaty work for us. Let others bleed as long as it is just on TV.

Imagine the world we could build if we had a dream?

If the artist in us was freed to worship and be?

Turn off the TV.

Put the phone down.

And go outside where there is no AC.

Demand from our leaders that we be set free.

Again.

Hooyah.

Memorial Day

Our flag flies at half-mast.

Our flag.

The flag of the United States of America.

Our flag allows us to debate, criticize and protest as much as we want without fear of persecution. It is amazing how much we love to criticize. Media and social networks are ablaze with condemnation. Oh yes, there are stories of good works… but those headlines are stolen by scandal and criticism, however intellectually cloaked.

Freedom of speech is the greatest threat to freedom throughout the world. What we take for granted is feared elsewhere. We are under attack by radical this and that because freedom of speech will destroy their power. Terrorism is applied to those willing to speak. Sad.

Graves freshly dug and graves of 1776 abound with sacrifice and tragedy. Tragedy is the life that was lost for no reason. Those of us who live have to make those losses have meaning by how we conduct ourselves. The veteran is not that outspoken for he knows the horror of war and the value of freedom. We all too often mock and abuse it.

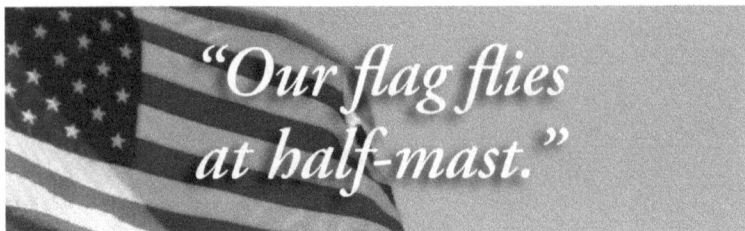

"Our flag flies at half-mast."

It is time we bring dignity and respect back into our lexicon. Yes ma'am, yes sir. Yes Mother, yes Father.

Our hypocrisy is so much more visible these days. Look at the killings and the excesses of our behavior. Look at pictures of crowds these days and how fat we have become. We mock those who differ. We mock religion... Respect for elders??? Forget it. They are just old people who are not relevant.

On Memorial Day we are bowing our heads to our cell phones and not to those who made this land of cell phones free.

The tear in the eye of the Veteran reflects the light of Truth.

It knows evil and it knows folly.

Thank you for your service.

Hooyah.

WTC

There are so many emergencies.

Men don't get it.

Small things can be extremely important too.

Who to call is a very perplexing decision.

Should it be a best friend? A fellow worker? Mom, but certainly not Dad… What about his parents?

One wrong decision on a WTC, "Who-To-Call"…. And it could really be a mess.

Life is a collaboration. It takes two people to make something happen. Going it alone most often ends in failure and disappointment. Not to test your thinking with another courts failure.

Two to tango, two to be family, two to be a marriage, a swim buddy to be a Navy SEAL.

Not having someone to consult is an insult to humanity. Why we even have a profession which is expanding greater than any other, consulting.

Our brain and being is also set up to be an Ego Palace, where self-reflection and self-adulation insures short term happiness and attention.

When one gives in to its allure, one becomes less important to others. People will quietly move away from you. Your insecurities will metastasize. There will be nobody to call. Your consultant will fall asleep because you are nothing but self.

Who to call? Not about the latest gossip. Mind you, I am not saying that calling your girlfriend about the observed behavior of another girlfriend is not fun. But let's leave fun for another time.

Who to call about the Truth? Who to call that you can trust?

Who really knows about what you need to know about?

It has to be someone who has experienced it. Not someone with an opinion, but someone who knows. Get it?

That is why your Who-To-Call is so important.

Your WTC has to be honest, humble, and value driven... Not fickle... One who knows right and wrong, good and bad. One who is not afraid to tell the Truth regardless of its impact on feelings.

Your WTC has to care more about others than self.

It sounds as if The WTC is not of this earth.

Hmmm.

Who to call?

Standing or kneeling?

Hooyah.

Instructor Waddell

I wrote a piece a while ago entitled PDTMWTD…

Please Don't Tell Me What To Do.

It was targeted at kids who don't like their parents telling them what to do… Well… and maybe it applies to husbands too??? You get the picture… any of us at any time. PDTMWTD.

When we tell someone what to do we are trying to warn them of possible consequences that we see that we think they don't see.

We all have to learn the same hard way; by experiencing and dealing with our own decisions. We want them to be ours. Why should we trust anyone else's opinion? "Enough with the advice!" we say. Of course, I am still saying that to my wife today….

Then… when we get a job we have to listen to our boss. Groan. If we really grow up we listen to our customers and clients, not ourselves. This is difficult, but it happens because it is paycheck driven. We listen and learn.

So it appears it is the incentive that is important. What is the incentive today when all kids withdraw into the self-assuring world of their cell phone? We are in trouble. They are affirmed by their insecure social network, not by our wisdom. They no longer "look up" to anything.

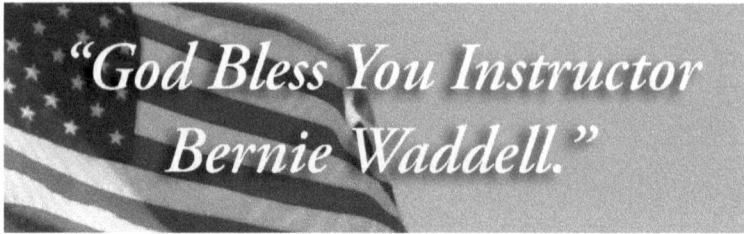

The word "No" is not allowed. Children are taught the nuances of "child abuse" and only have to tell their teachers and there will be a knock on the door.

I was blessed with great parents, spankings, and a plethora of "No's". Thank God.

But it was not until the military did I fully begin to appreciate what "No" meant. If you wanted to be a Navy Frogman/SEAL the INSTRUCTORS were waiting with snarling teeth and monstrous threats of pain. If you did not say "YES INSTRUCTOR" to everything they suggested there was a real price. Too many pushups, too many sit-ups, too many pull-ups, too many runs, too many swims… "Are they crazy?" I would think to myself. Is this nonsense really worth it? Why were they so strict? Why was my instructor Bernie Waddell so scary behind his wry smile?

Why??? Because all hell could rain down on you if you showed disrespect in any way, shape, or form. So just do what he asks and get on with your moment. Mile after mile crawling, running, and swimming in the freezing winter during Hell Week weeded out the non-survivors. The Yes Men.

You see… the instructors knew what would happen to you if you were not forged properly. You would be killed when it could have been avoided. Your swim buddy would have been put in peril unnecessarily. The mission aborted because you did not heed your instructor.

We need instructors in order to become all that we have the potential to become. Values must be honed in sweat and pain. We need to learn that freedom is not for free. If you are not conditioned, you will not be strong enough to stand in the winds of life. Laziness destroys potential.

There is white and black, good and evil, yes and no, do's and don'ts….

Values became valuable.

Serving others became more important than serving self.

Prayer became real.

Morality was affirmed.

God Bless You Instructor Bernie Waddell… and Godspeed.

And God Bless all the instructors everywhere.

And parents too.

Hooyah.

Fathers

Little girls love their Dads.

Little girls really need their Dads.

Dads define Moms.

Love is defined by Mom and Dad and how they look at each other.

As I am getting really old I am able to see things I never considered. Dynamics that shape security and insecurity, that hold back, and that empower.

I know more women now who were denied daughterhood. Dad left town or his work kept him away. Some in the military were deployed 80% of the year in not nice places doing not nice things. When back they had little time to build daughters or see their pleading eyes.

What is it like to not feel wanted? To not feel loved by a Dad? That is a special form of real abuse. It hurts. It hurts forever.

Dads are leaving town. Single parenthood is cancering our spirits and potential. Everybody is unhappy. The only road out of this town is forgiveness, for to understand why one was left without their Dad is mystifying. Dads are supposed to be the rock on which Mom's love nourishes.

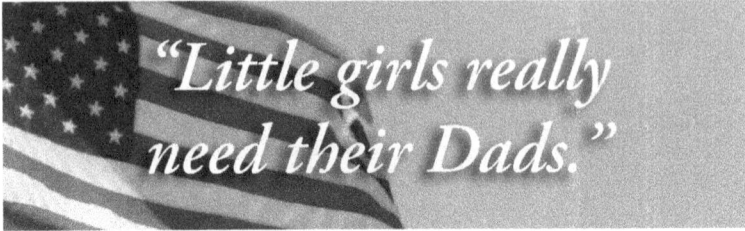

"Little girls really need their Dads."

There are those who had both parents leave. Total abandonment. A rotten card hand. They hid their pain. Some forgave without ever understanding. For some this fueled enormous success... driven to never let circumstance get the upper hand again. They won after really losing.

Recently, my Navy SEAL BUDS instructor from 50 years ago went to hospice after some years of declining health.

His daughters were always with him. They had discovered forgiveness the tough way.

Teammates from around the globe shared their stories and closeness to him with them.

A celebration of pain and love.

He found the Lord in his last years and had no fear.

On a Sunday, Master Chief Tom Blais left us in a quiet blaze of glory.

Fathers...

Hooyah.

Red Light District

I was at a red light last night, stopped of course…

And said to myself… Hmmm… This is funny…

Why is everybody next to me and across from me stopped??

Oh, yes, it is the red light.

It is just black and white.

The red light, that is.

Black and white.

Simple, no argument.

On red I don't go if I don't want to damage my beautiful car with someone crashing into it. Hmm… Black and white. Traffic rules. So I wait until green, look right and left and go without a scratch.

Why is it that these simple rules are so easily followed by us surging masses? Because we know what the consequences will be. This is the Red Light District. Where danger abounds for the foolhardy and self-appointed egos. I am in charge. I am in control. Except at the red light.

Well, you gotta know where I am going… Capiche?

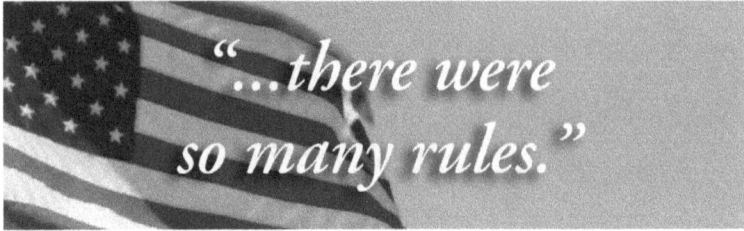

"...there were so many rules."

There are 10 ancient rules written on some dusty scrolls that I can't directly refer to because of political correctness. You know... those silly rules about killing, stealing, and other forms of irrational behavior.

Why does a red light have to be hanging on some pole at an intersection to help us not hurt ourselves?

You know, in the old days, for me the 50's and 60's, Mom and Dad laid down the laws. Hey, my parents loved me, well... at least what they hoped I could be... So I pretty much followed their rules. And lo and behold...whenever I went through their red lights I got in trouble. Funny. How could they be right and I be wrong? When I was a teenager I had right and wrong all figured out... and my parents were just wrong about things. Until I discovered otherwise...

What was cool about the Navy was that there were so many rules. So many "red lights". You can be sure you paid a price when you broke them.

Now in the SEAL training if you so much as winked it was an extra 50-100 pushups or a dip in the icy ocean and rolling in the sand and then some run up a stupid sand dune. You know what? You learned fast or failed. Failure sucks.

Red light? Black and white? Nope. Once again we have taken the liberty to take all that is black and white, or a red light, and turn it into grey so there is no decision to be made. All is now permissible as long as it is debatable…

Red light, green light… a game we used to play as kids. It was so much fun to follow the simple rules. Today… run the yellow and don't look back… and see the camera in your rear view mirror and worry for a week if the other bureaucracy will mail you a ticket.

Today the red light is the only red light we don't run. And we are blessed with single parents struggling to make it while we import all the drugs we can… Enough to feed the need for human disappointment in spite of the valiant efforts of interdiction forces, good guys putting their lives on the line.

 When will we have consequences again for ignoring the Black & White?

Why don't we treat our bodies and souls like we do our cars?

Have we turned our own neighborhoods into Red Light Districts?

Gotta go… Green light…

Hooyah.

The Camaraderie

It is the camaraderie.

One searches for truth and meaning under the guise of what makes one feel good.

There is entertainment, friendships, and all kinds of things which appear to be what life is.

Often these are devoid of purpose; just activities that make one feel good in the moment.

But, "Why am I here?" echoes deep within. Where do I make a difference? This is the man-quest. Women have birth and family. Man searches. Man succumbs to aloneness and journeys that lead nowhere. There is pain without purpose.

Military veterans come home and bring their private pain and surface smiles. Many have seen the belly of the beast. But it is the basic training and living together as brothers with tomorrow's uncertainties that forges a bond unimagined by civilians, by families even.

Eating and sleeping, often in extremely difficult circumstances.

Never knowing the closeness of the unseen enemy.

"It's the damned camaraderie, stupid."

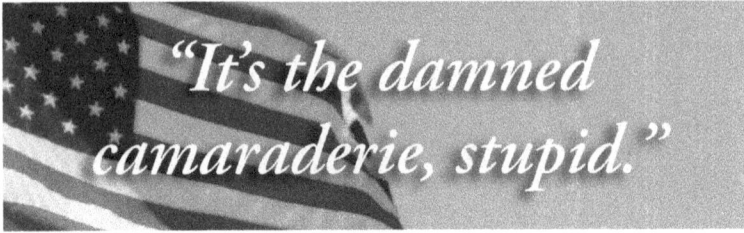

There is always a mission and purpose to the next day… even if it is just to take care and be with your buddies, your brothers in cammo.

The meaning of your life is defined and private prides are worn.

Then you embark from the returning aircraft and receive the hugs of family.

No one knows what your eyes have seen.

They want you back as before.

You are not the same.

They can't get it. Only your buddies can who are spread far and wide from states to cemeteries.

Finding a job is often hard. Employers have no shared experience. They have no clue as to the disciplines and focus you have experienced. They are the amateurs in life, but don't know it. You have graduated, but don't know it.

Manhood comes from the camaraderie of combat; of getting close to evil. From being next to a buddy's last breath. From touching an artificial limb.

One had learned to communicate without sound. Eye contact rules…

Caring for a buddy more than one's self.

It's the damned camaraderie stupid.

Hire a veteran.

You owe it to yourself.

Hooyah.

Lone Survivor

A mother is standing on a hill grasping the hands of her two small children.

Divorce.

Single parenthood.

A tear unseen.

A choice is weighing down on her soul.

There is a path of short term relief with substances and unnamed people. But those two pairs of hands...??? To quit or to go forward into the unknown, putting those tiny palms ahead of her own.

We cannot predict the future but we can shape it with each positive, unselfish step. Faith yielding hope. One step at a time.

On a lonely mountain in Afghanistan 4 Navy SEALs chose not to kill a shepherd and a child. A choice. You may have read the book or seen the movie. Lone Survivor. Intense. They became trapped. A young man stood high atop a rock to try to get his SAT phone to transmit his team's location. He was killed. Lt. Mike Murphy fell there forever. His mother left alone on that hill in spirit with him. One Lone SEAL survived. His name is Marcus. He survived to tell the story with grace.

"Mike's mother cried that day."

Young women get pregnant.

They no longer know if they will be left on the hill.

What has become of us?

If a fetus could talk would she have second thoughts, in this, our celebrated 21st century? Would she pack it in?.... "Forget it. I don't want to be a burden to my future mother. Save a lot of money on skinny jeans"....

What is happening to our men? The notion of responsibility and commitment appears to have been terminated with prejudice by questionable social forces. Where does a young man go for direction? We have even found a way to neuter the Boy Scouts.

Make mistakes and all you get is sensitivity therapy and the assignment of blame to someone or something else. Where is the man walking back up that hill to take the hands of his woman and children? Is the hill too steep? Is not the reward obvious? Ride up on your four-wheeler and load them all on board and get back to being a parent....

Where are the leaders and politicians? Isn't this the terminal cancer in our society? Roman Empire all over again?

The noise of politicians accusing and complaining is heard all across our nation.... like two parents in the final throws of divorce? The family, the heart of our country, will inherit this empty void. This is a bullet at close range.

Forget global warming. What about the erosion of motherhood and family and values? What do we value any more?

Can someone in Washington give us some values to value? The Constitution is a good place to look. Why did they bother to write it? And agree?

There is also The Book....

Mike's mother cried that day.

Her son was cool.

He cared more for others.

He never got to have any children.

He still died for them.

2,000 years ago a mother named Mary cried.

Hooyah.

Dirty Name

When you get angry and swear you call someone a dirty name.

Not nice, but you just have to before, or if, you hit them.

A fight could ensue if you kept it all within and did not do something.

So a dirty name is the sign of uncontrolled emotion and anger.

Say it and you will feel better??

However… however, the receiver of this compliment might be offended and call you one… or even better… take a swing at you.

Politicians call the other party dirty names though they are more eloquent and oblique. They have their own code language.

Nations do the same when their representatives are interviewed on CNN. We get it. They show restraint, but we know the otherwise. There are nations which foster evil plain and simple. They don't deserve a dirty name. They deserve an economic bomb at the least. Some need a real one dropped from the sky. Have we not learned that violence doesn't respond to aspirin?

There is an obstacle called the Dirty Name in Coronado California and Little Creek Virginia. It is well known by all SEALs. You look at it and

"Say it and you will feel better??"

swear. How are you going to attack it? You walk up to it to size it up on your first visit. An instructor explains the goal… to leap to the first log landing on your stomach then the same to the top one. Except they are a little too high. You swear. You call it anything vulgar. It will require total commitment. Big gamble to leap that far and that high. It is an S.O.B. …… You see someone else struggle ahead of you and fall off. Attempt again. Attempt again. Get threatened and humiliated by the instructor.

Dig deep and hurl yourself into the unknown and make it.

Life throws curves.

Life is all obstacles if you choose to look at it that way.

So many quit, get depressed, or avoid what is directly in their path.

Seize every moment and overcome with Faith.

Hooyah

Command Authority

Who the hell is in charge here?

Here?

Where?

Washington?

No dummy, who is in charge here?

Okay, here are some "here"s.

Let's say we are in Italy in a small family home and mamma is bringing out the spaghetti to her family table. All are anxious to eat. Who do you think is in charge?

Okay, now to a farm in Kansas. Dad and his sons are finishing up the day and the dinner bell rings. Who do you think is in charge?

Mom. Mothers are always in charge. AKA Wife. It works, it always has worked.

Okay, now to the city. Let's pick a poor family. Detroit. Mom works. Dad left a long time ago. Kids stay in school as long as possible. Their peers are in charge. Their cellphone is in charge. Mom comes home and cooks as best she can. She is in charge, kinda…??

What was good about the Navy was that there was always someone in

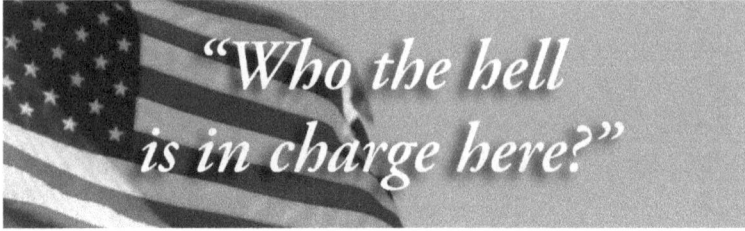

"Who the hell is in charge here?"

charge. Someone in charge of most everything…. And… It was all written down too. No doubt about right and wrong. Regulations galore. And guess what? Everybody is happy including the twenty year olds. Go figure?

We need a command authority to be organized and to be happy. Getting back to swearing….. What the hell has happened?

Wherever the father is missing there is trouble. On the farms at dinner most Dads are quiet as Mom is boss. We men wait to have our jollies out in the fields. But it is good to have Dad at the table. His deference to Mom creates the authority she needs. Values can be discussed. The day can be shared. Nice. Healthy. The way it should be.

Enter the keyboard, heads down. Not in prayer but in text keystroke. All is lost. The new ruler is the instant gratification of the "click".

Dads have to come back and help Mom say no.

All cellphones go in the bowl at dinner.

My buddy Vann told me he does that with his 4 boys.

May I have some more beans Mom?

Hooyah.

Spare Rod

"Hey Bob, do you have a spare rod?"

"No I don't Rich… they have a decent selection at Ace Hardware…"

(An hour later at Ace)…. "Tell me about your rods. What are the most popular?"

Sales Associate… "I have this long flexible thin one and this shorter thicker one that are hard to keep in stock".

"Tell me more"

"Well, the long thin one really stings but leaves no marks while the shorter thick one does bruise a bit, but is more efficient".

Spare the rod and spoil the child.

Worked for centuries say most of the men in the room. Of course they are older and not social-networking proficient.

Concern for feelings has replaced the rod. And our kids know we care about their feelings. They feel cared for to a new degree. They feel their feelings entitle them to more and more pleasing interactions with life.

Just mouthing the words… "That is Wrong Ken!" does not convince

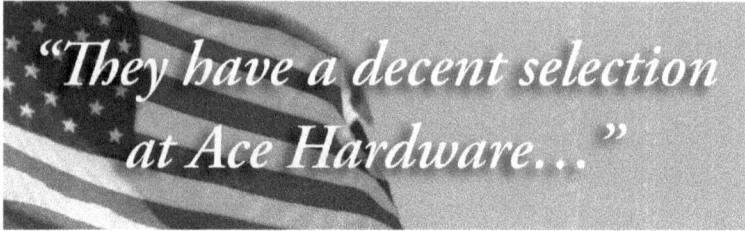
"They have a decent selection at Ace Hardware..."

Ken otherwise. But take him out to the woodshed and he will thank you 40 years later. What is important to our parents is important to us.

Life can be real cruel if you are not resilient and strong enough to endure the pain. To heck with feelings when the moment is critical. Action is required regardless of "feelings" by-products.

Fighting for good takes no prisoners.

Spare not the rod and spare not the bomb if evil is taking our youth hostage. Damn it, you can't have them! They belong to us. They belong to the Good.

Put on your Evil Vision Goggles world! .... and pull triggers on these philosophical clowns.

They don't have to see you.

Just plant seeds and start saying "NO" again.

Put the cell phones in a basket at dinner.

Fill the umbrella stands with rods....

Hooyah.

Mosul Dam

Dam it.

Build a dam with thousands of workers and engineers.

River water will back up and provide life for farms and towns and families. Dams make futures. Destroy the dam and you will be destroyed.

High stakes poker.

Where is the red line America?

When are the weak protected by the strong? I hope they are in my home town, my church, or my "hood".

I have to be willing to fight for something.

Evil is not going away with words.

Dam it.

Damn it.

Hooyah.

50th Reunion

Every one of us should be blessed to live long enough to have a 50th Reunion for something.

Be it High School, College, Surf Club, or having experienced something special with someone.

The passage of 50 years gives one the perspective of age to savor the good and the bad.

Your unique life journey and personality are refined in the passage of 50 years. You can wink with your reunion mates and know....

In 50 years so many go such different paths that you have little in common. Those from 50 years ago are not relevant.... But they are poignant. They are part of you as you were being formed. They are special, they are precious, they are part of your miraculous uniqueness.

BUDS (UDTR) Class 31E graduated in July of 1964. It was a winter class. An East Coast class in Little Creek, VA. There was some snow and ice to savor. Hell Week is a blur now and my aging classmates are giving up little detail.

Hell Week is kind of like life. You have no clue what to expect and you

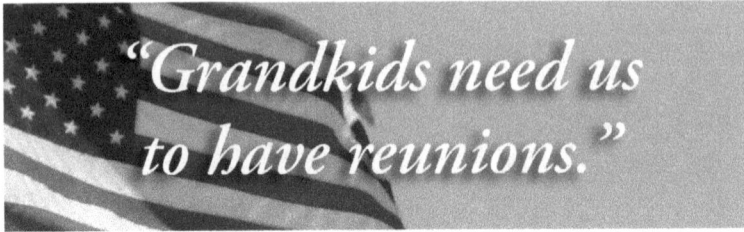

learn one thing. Not quitting does get you somewhere regardless of your occupation or problem.

We only met briefly at a dinner with wives. We had no opportunity to cocoon up and share. I'd like to know them as men. Their journeys. Not meant to be.

We were all UDTs then a few were SEALs after a while.... Then later all UDTs became SEALs. The Trident the standard for all. We did not think we were anything special back then. The military was being denigrated in the media. Many came back from Vietnam to be greeted with the emptiness of public disdain.

Good guys trying to do good. No such thing as "Thank you for your service". Nothing. But a reunion is still rich with knowledge of a fabulous bond that is shared by any sharing stress for a long period.

This is the mettle of families. This is what we fight for... to protect the family so it can be safe and free to be itself. To teach understanding and respect and honesty...

Family reunions are the best. Kids love to see a grandparent hugging their adult child...

Grandkids need us to have reunions.

They need to see that happy endings are possible.

Social networking should complement reunion, not replace it.

Even 70 year olds can still make a difference.

Godspeed Class 31E.

Hooyah.

Mr. Murphy.

This will be the only title with a period in it.

That is to make special significance of this subject.

It must be taken seriously??

I bet many of you do not know who Mr. Murphy is. Especially our younger generations.

Mr. Murphy is the CEO of Conceit. His corporation's Mission Statement is referred to by the educated as "Murphy's Law". "Anything that can go wrong will go wrong."

In the SEALs this is accepted as the vital center of all planning. Reducing risk. The more you reduce it the better the chances of coming back alive.

Coming back alive? Hmmm? If you choose to look back on your life look at all the times something went wrong, or something that you said had the wrong effect. Aren't there things you wish you could take back? "If I only had just done…"

I think of the people I have hurt by saying something I thought funny too quickly. Or things that invisibly hurt others. Can't change it now. One can only go forward with a new knowledge of what not to do next

"Coming back alive?"

time. Some call this wisdom. Others humility.

Mr. Murphy does not give a damn about you. He only cares that our thinking is faulty. He is the one who is Laughing Out Loud....

As we learn to laugh at ourselves and accept our limitations, we begin to have value.

Dangerous jobs or relationships require focus on what can go wrong. Everything you do at work requires no mistakes. Everything you say to your spouse requires delicacy and sincerity. The same for your children. Mr. Murphy pretends he is a kid and plays alongside them too.

As I write this I have to be careful that Mr. Murphy isn't encouraging me to say the wrong thing.

Better end it now before he does.

Hooyah.

Sure You Can

I don't know classical music at all.

I remember the Lone Ranger radio show and its William Tell Overture…. That's sadly it.

The Everly Brothers, the Kingston Trio, and the Beatles killed any chance of classical surviving, much less opera. No, not Oprah dummy…..

Yet people in large quantities have never let go of the classical. It is a pure art form in music…. And not the Picasso-ization of popular music.

We watch The Voice and these struggling vocalists make it to national TV and its grand rejections to find the winner. Some came back from prior years because a Pharrell Williams, or Blake Shelton etc…. may have said "Sure you can." Go back and work harder.

We all need to hear "sure you can" more often and we desperately need to encourage others the same way.

Sure you can get that job.

Sure you can feel better.

Sure you can climb that mountain.

"I don't know classical music at all."

Sure you can have better manners....

Let's see which of us can make the longest list of "Sure You Can's."

I say to all you young wannabe SEALs.... Sure You Can!

If you shook hands with every new graduate of BUDS (*Basic Underwater Demolition Seal*) school... you would say he looks just like me... or did several years ago... a scrawny kid with pimples....

You see, you have to work very hard and long to condition yourself to achieve all goals. Every real rich person was poor once.

Nothing of value is effort free.

It is the *not giving up spirit* in spite of the "it's not worth it" wall that everyone faces. Quitting just takes saying "I quit. This is not for me." and ringing life's bell.

Yet one failure can lead to a different success. It is all a question of attitude, spirit, and sense of humor. Sure you can.

Someone on the piano this morning at church was playing some classical piece. I thought this guy was real good. A student? I looked at the program. *Impromptu No. 4 G flat major by Franz Schubert*. Now this is the real deal folks. I strained to see the pianist. A young, neat looking, black man.

All I could think was "Sure You Can."

He has already played in Carnegie Hall.

Wow, I got to hear him play today.

"Sure you can."

Hooyah.

Muslim Sunglasses

Do you know they are making sunglasses that work with the burqa?

You can hardly see the eyes as it is.

Talk about becoming mysterious…. More dark, more intriguing.

What is the point of being a woman if no one can look at you?

When there is bright sun and SPF is required, the sunglass industry is right there for any price you wish to pay. Try a Chanel for $300? Why?? Do you really see better? I think sunglasses are more fashion than required, unless of course you are climbing Mt Everest or flying an F35 into the dawn.

Tints make what one sees unnatural. It is like we don't want to see things for what they really are. N'est-ce pas??

We are being drawn into cultural assimilations that just are not the U. S. of A. Talk about a clash of cultures!!! Beverly Hills bikinis vs. burqas in a steel cage match. Nothing to grab on the LA Divas, and everything to grab on the champion burqa feline. You can't train in a burqa… but you can do everything in a bikini.

What in the world are we going to do with this Muslim thing?

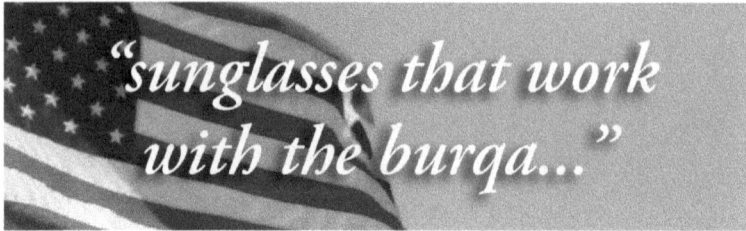
"sunglasses that work with the burqa..."

I know we are supposed to be politically correct. But radical Islam is giving the whole Muslim world a bad image. Really bad. Fear is their weapon and we are afraid of fear. Ask us to be forgiving… we like to forgive.

But WWII started off just this way. It took Churchill and Roosevelt to face fear's ugly face and give us resolve and hope.

Our worlds came together. Evil had united us. Good won. Nobody tried to avoid the draft.

What are we looking for from our government? Yes we run there more and more these days to solve all our problems. They can only come up with legislation.

Haven't we all had enough with legislation?

There is so much that only an extra-terrestrial can figure it out.

Maybe we all should wear a burqa so the bad guys can't see us?

Are there any 6 foot burqas?

I'm gonna wear sunglasses too.

Hooyah.

Pay Scale

What is the correct hourly wage for a woman?

Why do we act as if gender does not exist?

Man provides.

It is in his caveman DNA.

But has he over-interpreted his mandate?

Today's world is more merit based… hopefully. The culture is changing. Technology driven work is gender indifferent and it will dominate soon. A woman should not be a Navy SEAL, but most everything else looks open going forward. (I'm also against them being in combat; too bad…)

With some real thinking and maybe a dose of compassion I have come to the conclusion that women are better suited for more kinds of work than has ever been considered. They are tough on detail. They can be more determined. They can be more ethical. In being Mothers, they have been battle tested in their own battlefields. They have to fight for values and nurture at the same time.

I used to get hazardous duty pay, jump pay, demolition pay. Mothers who work should get child care pay. Not to enable, but to respect. Not

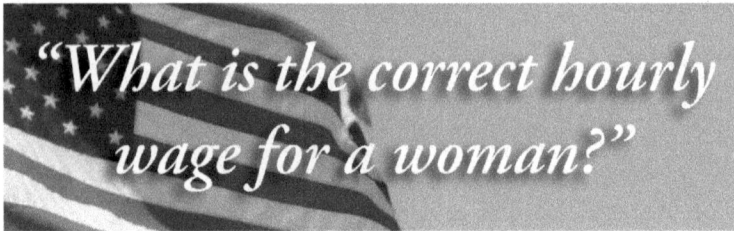

"What is the correct hourly wage for a woman?"

to have more children, but to respect the service she truly provides.

There is a fairness issue here. Think about it.

Men are as moody as women. Men can be equally smart and equally dumb. Times are a-changing and women deserve and are going to get better. The time has come where we must work alongside with equal opportunity and pay.

It is we men who have to show more respect and learn to dump all chauvinist thoughts.

I know.

My wife is my boss.

She makes a lot more than me.

Hooyah.

Ice Water

If you cut a hole in the ice in the middle of a lake, build your shelter, and sit with your son with your lines going down into the ice water….. Do you think about what in the heck could live there??

Fish.

Cold blooded fish.

Kinda crazy.

And we know that there are cold blooded evil people and governments that think nothing about killing. They have to be dealt with. Not ignored.

Sanctions are fine, but sometimes a trigger is required. Drones are sloppy, telescopic sights are better. It takes bravery and courage to get that close.

Dumping buckets of ice water on the heads of celebrities for a noble cause accomplished its mission. I am sure they were chilly and inconvenienced for a brief moment. But there are even more significant noble causes that just do not grab our attention; women's and child abuse are at the top. Poverty. Evil… Just plain evil.

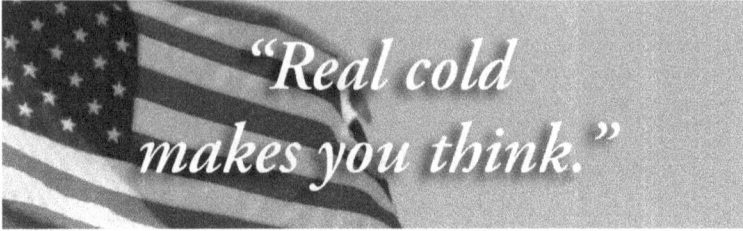

"Real cold makes you think."

Only churches are allowed to talk about evil. It is a taboo word outside of those walls. Crazy…when our #1 problem is evil. We just assign it other names so it fades away into politically correct irrelevancy.

Real cold makes you think.

I remember trying to get our rubber boat (IBL Inflatable Boat Large) over an ice covered rock jetty in a snow storm in February 1964. Now that was SEAL training. Now that was evil. Made for good swearing, though… You don't want to know real cold. The ice bucket isn't real cold.

Ever read Nathaniel Hawthorne's The Scarlet Letter??

Maybe each of us should carry an ice water bucket around with us all day. When we start to think about doing something selfish, inconsiderate, or ever so slightly evil… we should stop and dump the bucket on our head as a reminder for all to see...

A reminder that every time we sin our world gets colder.

Hooyah.

EPCER 857

USS MARYSVILLE EPCER 857.

They sent me there as my first duty station in the Navy after college and OCS.

It wasn't what this 22 year old wanted.

Sometimes we have to do things we don't want…

You couldn't refuse or say "whatever" back then.

Experimental Patrol Craft Escort Rescue….. She was stationed out of the US Naval Electronics Laboratory on Pt. Loma, San Diego. I came aboard on Jan 1, 1963.

You see, the Navy had decided that potential Naval Special Warfare Officers, UDT/SEAL, needed some real shipboard experience before they became "special". Reputations as cowboys and independent behavior needed a solution.

So we towed a 500 foot thermistor chain at 5 knots between Acapulco and San Francisco for a year getting temperature versus depth data. Slow and boring?? Not really as you were always busy on the 184 ft. steel ship. Some big storms way out there all alone. Learned a little about how Navy things worked. It was good.

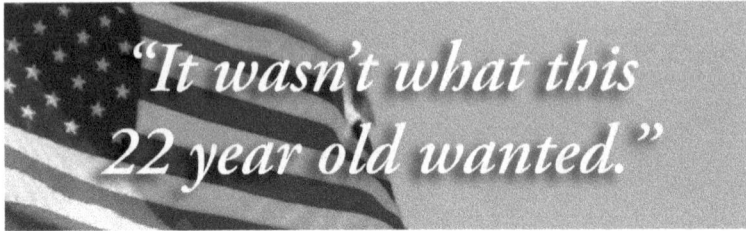

I left and reported into UDT/SEAL Training, aka BUDS on Jan 2, 1964. Winter Class. It got cold. The Chesapeake got nasty. Hell Week was nasty. It all was such a shock that you didn't have time to digest food or what was happening. I wouldn't quit. I learned to laugh and swear and to trust.

But this is about having to go places you don't want to. This is about learning from every experience. Every experience makes you more unique. You won't know until years later what it was all about. How you were forged by good times and bad times. When we are young we are so ignorant and arrogant. Our opinions are so off base, pun intended, that it is a miracle we survive.

Maybe EPCER 857 taught me things I needed to know. Maybe I would have quit BUDS without that experience. I have no clue. But do any of us?

The lesson is to forge ahead, one day at a time, sorting right from wrong.

Easy from hard.

Not quitting.

Finding trust.

Taking orders.

Following rules.

Holding out your hand to the one reaching towards yours.

Always willing to help.

5 Knots is not so bad if you get where you are going and bring back something of value.

Hooyah.

RWE

Romeo Whiskey Echo.

Are we happy?

Are we having a good time?

Are we making a difference?

Or are we just worrying about self?

Are we fighting any battle that means something?

Are we trying to help stop the arguing?

Who would have thought that the letters RWE could pose so many questions? They almost ask us if we ask ourselves enough questions. What about our youth? Are they being asked the right questions? And more important are they being held accountable for their answers?? Or their actions?

Are there enough laws to insure that all actions are correct? And to what end? Laws used to be about what is good. Now they are drifting towards the political correctness of feelings. Fairness only exists when feelings are not hurt. The new paradigm.

With our political system looking like chaos to the rest of the world

"Romeo Whiskey Echo."

we are no longer presenting the democratic model of efficiency and rightness. Right used to be what is good. We all used to agree on what was good. There was the right way and the wrong way and children were taught it. History was without bias. Religion was respected.

Are we ignoring evil? It seems as if using that word makes you a reactionary. Yet evil is more manifest than ever. It should be more contained than ever. What happened? Can't we even discuss it??

Since when is a spade a heart?

What have we given up on?

Are we sleeping in or are we in a pew on Easter morning?

Are we who we were meant to be?

RWE?

Right Wing Extremist?

Hooyah.

Sea Legs

Sea legs is an old nautical term that describes someone new coming on board and the time it took to adapt to the rhythm and rolling of the ship in heavy seas.

It is, at first, tough to maintain your balance when every axis moves. There are smells and sounds all of which can make one seasick.

Heck, even some of you landlubbers can get sick on a cruise ship doing nothing but sailing smoothly along. I remember some very stormy rough plunging days on a small ship in the pacific. I was new, and up on the conn it was a roller coaster. But the throwing up soon ceased as I got my sea legs.

We all think we know more than we do. You think you know as much as your boss until you have 10 years under your belt and you realize there was more to learn.

Try and tell teenagers they don't know what they are talking about. They have sea legs for nothing.

Now one would think cell phones are so easy. That facebook is so easy. That twitter is so easy. And on and on. But even these require sea legs!! Over time one makes mistakes in saying something one shouldn't have

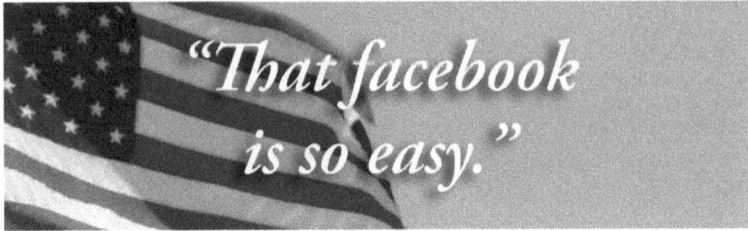

"That facebook is so easy."

to someone you shouldn't have. Copying someone by mistake. Several times I wanted to throw up. I wasn't careful about what I was doing. I didn't have my social networking sea legs!

It is human nature to assume one knows more than one does. As you get older, and as you get really older, you see things you never did 5 years prior. Age is kind of sea legs.

How about what one knows about what is right and wrong?

How about what to do about evil or…. Unfairness?

How about knowing when to just act without further discussion.

How about setting one's own lines in the sand?

In the sea of life, sea legs means knowing that helping others is the only thing that can keep you from heaving over the side……

Hooyah.

Something Fishy

Sometimes something just feels not right.

Premonition?

Or just a private suspicion that something is fishy....

Feel that way about the world?

There is so much poverty and violence and it is now the 21st century! We have put man on the moon and an apple on our wrist. What gives?

The fishing boat goes out into the ocean and brings back a magnificent catch. Offloads and gets a great price for the 5,000 lbs. of tuna. The Japanese really pay for quality tuna. But the boat smells fishy. Really hard to get that smell out. You could if you wanted to.....

Why in the USA are there so many poor? We can understand Africa and the Middle East... but the USA?

Admittedly we have been nourishing an entitlement subculture, but there is more to it than that.

The rich are getting richer they say... Our financial institutions have fees on transactions that insure few walk away with more. Why does a

hedge fund manager or even broker get paid so much for phone calls promoting us gambling on "sure" things? The art of the deal?

Workers still provide the product and seldom share in these profits. Something is fishy. We are a nation, a democracy that is a family of the Constitution of fairness and justice. The rich really can afford to do with less. They would still be creative and productive with half their incomes.

There are companies that truly respect the employee and really take care of them. Unions aren't needed when there is honesty and true appreciation of the contribution every employee makes.

We have tiered ourselves into inefficient structured bureaucracies where supervisor reports to supervisor who reports to supervisor. Fertile ground for politics??

How often does the CEO go into his trenches and shake the hands of the supervised?

Who praises whom and how... and when??

In WWII factories sprang up all across the nation to produce war materials. 500 bombers a day. And we felt good. And most everyone had an honest job.

There was no money being skimmed by financial fishermen....

Values were different then. That war had to be won. We are the beneficiaries. Yet we have also enabled the next war by not keeping our values intact.

Values in the boardroom and values in the home.

Have we created the greatest Ponzi scheme of them all?

Pretending we are found when we are lost?

Something is fishy.

I sure love the Swan River Fish Restaurant across the street.

Hooyah.

Toy Soldiers

The drums of war are from afar.

Always from afar.

We can't hear them because we have the Atlantic and Pacific foam soundproofing.

We have our ear buds stuck in tight with our heads lowered into our cellphones. No problems. No worries. Whatever. Headphones have made us headphonies.

Our best young have donned uniforms and been driven into shape by discipline and training. They will board planes and ships and with gusto insert themselves into the abyss of evil and pain.

Elected by us, politicians debate when to send them and how to support them. Herein our soldiers have become toys. Generals are forced to become consensus executives. Against their instincts, they have been forced into sending the innocent abroad, with perilous timing into perilous circumstances.

The best defense being the offense has become inverted. It is now the era where the best offense is defense. It's more like the NFL than dead serious conflict.

"The drums of war are from afar."

You have to believe there is evil to fight it. You have to believe in the concept of good and evil. That a child is good. That a child's future is worth dying for. Mothers do.

Values are no longer taught in classrooms. Nor on the cell phone. Social networking has become a party of avoidance. Stimulating the entitlement senses.

War is becoming more inevitable. It is looming on the horizon.

The ships and planes carrying our soldiers are not toys. 9MM guns are not toys. They are meant to do one thing only. To kill. Why? Why?? To keep from being killed.

This is no Sony Play Station.

The blood is warm. The bandages are not found on the remote.

Our toy soldiers are not plastic.

They carry photo ID's and letters to home.

Look up America and search the Heavens for direction.

Thanks Doc.

Hooyah.

27,000 Pages

When I was a kid, things were pretty simple.

If Johnny said something mean to me I just hit him and that was the end of it.

I then grew a bit and got my Kentucky driver's license, signed one form, drove the test… and was free for life!

There was a thing called the handshake back then. It worked for most agreements. I wasn't old enough for a job or taxes. Life was easy to understand. There weren't many lawyers.

I went in the Navy and my income tax form was really simple as pie. You could figure it out… maybe two to three pages, a deduction, and you got a check. This worked for a long time. I got out and it still was a non-event. Your company supplied your W-2, you deducted your mortgage stuff, some charity, and put a stamp on the envelope.

It was a little more for a small business, but the accountant had it figured out.

Fast forward. Today's tax code is 27,000 pages. The fine print tries to outwit the payee. Every possible interpretation is potentially covered in infinite fine print. Hello??? Tilt!!!

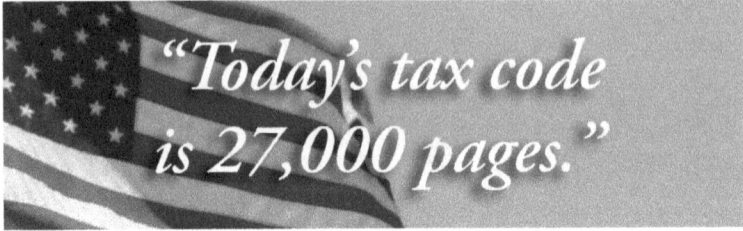

How did this happen? Who is to blame? This is evil. This is bureaucracy gone wild. Where are the Bureaucracy Police? Where is transparency?

It has been stabbed in the aorta by keyboards and fine print. Is this really government protecting us or is it white collar crime on the grandest scale? Where are the environmental watchdogs? This is our economic environment that is being strangled by an administrative shell game.

Who writes this stuff anyway? Who signs off on it? Isn't it time to say "Throw the bums in jail!"?

Every government says they are going to make things simple and they lie to us. Remember the 9-9-9 concept? It may have been brilliant with a few adjustments, but NOT 27,000 pages worth!!!

We need SEAL politicians who will not quit or flinch in the face of fully armed special interest attorneys. It is time to "just do it." Chuck it all.

And now that we have a concept… How about applying it to the deficit? The budget. The entitlements. Make a bill a bill with no attachments, no pork, no special interest addendums. Make everything stand on its own. Just do it.

Well, maybe this postulating is too late.

Maybe 27,000 pages have sealed our fate and the cliff is here.

I see the top of the waterfall 100 yards ahead.

The noise… aghhh… See ya.

Hooyah.

3-Foot World

You want to get something done??

You want to climb the face of Yosemite's El Capitan?

You want to be a Navy SEAL and finish the impossible swim?

You want to be a mother giving birth?

There is a secret. Stop the worry. Stop the second guessing. Stop the feelings.

Laugh. Yes laugh. Find humor in the moment. Search for it. Seize it. Laugh out loud! Say something ridiculous.

We are laughing at all the wrong things these days. At others. At politicians. At authority. Even at good.

The funniest thing to laugh at is you. Yes, you, yourself. Only you know how funny you are!!

Kick, stroke, kick, stroke, kick, stroke……. If you had to think about how many in a 7 mile swim you would quit. Most everyone quits in life. And they quit by laughing at others when they should be laughing at themselves. God gave us humor to humor ourselves and to help others get through their trials.

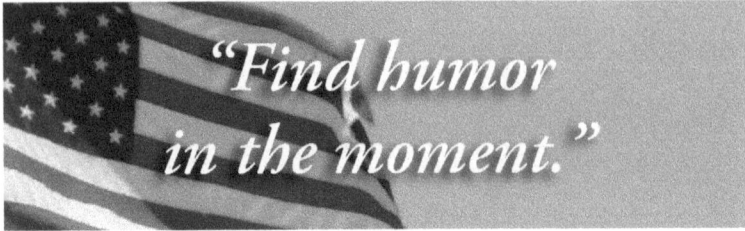

"Find humor in the moment."

This can only happen in your 3-foot world. That is in the moment. Your moment to seize… one moment at a time. How often I said "What the heck am I doing here??" and kept plodding on. Now for weeks, then months, then years at a time. Lots to laugh at.

Worry sucks.

Worry saps all your energy.

Worry steals your individuality…. And your personality.

Stay in your 3-foot zone and you can climb any mountain, fingers bleeding… with a smile.

Rock on.

Hooyah.

South Pole

The North Pole is cold and barren.

The ocean below is 13,000 feet deep.

The South Pole is really cold and barren.

It has mountains.

You don't want to live there.

You can only stay warm at the North Pole in a nuclear submarine.

You can stay warm at the South Pole in the McMurdo Sound Station, Antarctica.

Life is cruel at the poles.

Now in between the water is warm and the weather is good, though a little hot at the equator.

There is only so far north you can go and there is only so far south you can go. Your choice. In either case these extremes do not offer safe haven.

Maybe there is an analogy between the left and the right?

It sure seems like we are all trying to pick a pole to live on. Democrat or Republican. Polarized. Frozen in time. Cold to reason. Cold to compromise. Cold to agreement. Cold to love.

"You don't want to live there."

The world is the same. Extremes fighting normality. Evil basking in the void of polarizations. Evil cannot be brought to justice if those who are good are not united.

God didn't create us to live on the poles…. Our bodies may still be in the USA but our politics are way out there in accusation land. Senate or Congress, it is freezing in there. So many well-intentioned, corrupted by the winds of power and money swirling in confusing vortexes across their chambers. A maelstrom of moral chaos. Maybe this is just life as it is.

Our planet is no more than it is. The poles couldn't be further away. But it is all so awesome. From sub-atomic particles to the stars in the sky. From the pulse of our being to the compassion in our heart.

It is time to write down what is valuable to us.

Like our forefathers on July 4, 1776.

United we stand.

Divided we fall.

Hooyah.

Orion to Earth

A United Launch Alliance Delta 4 Heavy rocket launched the unmanned Orion deep space capsule on December 5, 2014.

Someday it will take man to Mars.

Apollo was the father of Orion.

Apollo took 3 men to the moon.

Look at the heights of man.

A profound accomplishment.

What am I going to do with you earth? What to do??

Why are your heads looking down all the time to keyboards? Don't you see what is going on around you? The world is a total mess. Evil and selfishness are sapping you of all your potential.

You look so beautiful with your blue seas and white clouds and your green and brown land masses.

For thousands of years you have been fighting.

For thousands of years you have been abusing women.

For thousands of years you have been abusing children and animals.

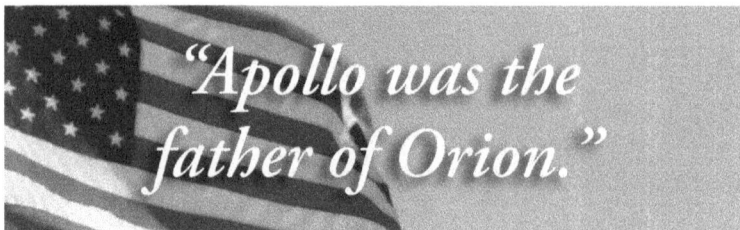

"Apollo was the father of Orion."

It does not look like you even know the difference.

Are the heavens the only escape? Do we have to populate another planet to start all over the right way? What commandments will we use as our cornerstones there?

How can man be so great and so abhorrent at the same time?

Astronauts get to float around and hold hands.

No politics allowed here.

Why?

Why are they smiling and taking pictures of us?

What do they know that we don't?

Hooyah.

Mal Ad Osteo

There is no such thing as good alone.

For us good is best defined by evil.

It is sad that what is bad has to preoccupy us.

We all avoid getting hurt. Hurt means pain. Bad always brings pain.

When evil lurks… when evil people get close only bad happens.

History shows us that man cannot escape the evil forces in this world. Who the hell knows why. But… to just look the other way means evil thrives and consumes more innocent and good lives.

Texting will not make evil go away. Evil knows how to tweet now.

What does it take for evil to be defeated or at least checked??

It takes a military willing to go to the front lines and say "NO!"

Yet in our country today we look at the military almost as a necessary evil…. This is crazy. Our young men are being softened by fathers who do not make them strong. Men make men.

Whatever your role in the military may be, you are making the machine to support those who go out into the dark fringes of the impossible to risk all for us.

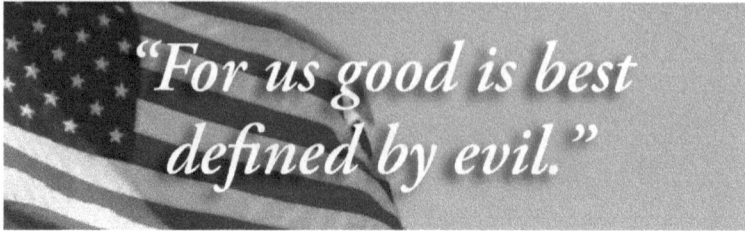
"For us good is best defined by evil."

We have a motto "Mal Ad Osteo".

It translates to "Bad To The Bone".

What could that possibly mean?

How much effort does it take a really good guy to fight evil for us?

I'd say all the effort that he can muster. In fact, he has to be better trained and have a greater, more solid idealism than the bad guys. He has to instill fear too. Those who are evil have to know they are fighting an enemy with enormous resolve, that though fair, they are "Bad To The Bone".

We all need to reconsider how we approach evil in our family and in our schools and in our nation. Call it what you may, there are forces at play that are robbing our youth of their manhood and their integrity and their potential.

Sometimes we may have to be "Bad To The Bone" there too.

How bad is it to say "NO"?

Hooyah.

American Sniper

American Sniper is a movie made from a book by a real person.

It is biographical non-fiction.

The author was murdered.

Chris Kyle was a good man.

A very good man.

His murderer was sick and evil and one of us.

This movie is proving to be one of the all-time largest grossing films.

All the competition are fantasy fiction movies.

All are pure entertainment and escapes from reality. Escapes.

American Sniper is not.

Its greatness and appeal is from confronting issues head on with artistic realism. We are forced into conversations that all other movies avoid. What to do about evil? Who can do something about it? Does evil exist? We get criticized if we try to define what is good or bad. Sad state of affairs.

The movie makes us think about what military families give up for

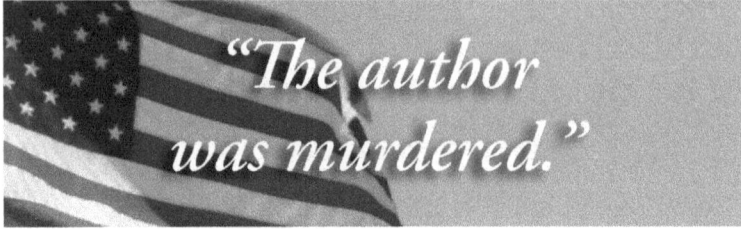

"The author was murdered."

us. The movie provides moral dilemmas facing the soldier. It is not impersonal but personal. Memories haunted by acts of horror and doubt.

We have Navy SEALs to do some special assignments in the quiet. Risk taking at the extreme. Beyond conventional boundaries. Special Warfare is special. Training is beyond imagination. Others know nothing about it.

The movie misses giving us a real feeling of the exhaustion and pain endured. Hell week is a week of indescribable fortitude and compromise. You have to give up your being to trust. Trust that you will not die. You may quit at any time. A choice that terrifies you every moment.

Leaders are forged.

They know what it takes.

Moral leadership requires moral leadership.

The world needs us.

"Quitting is not an option."

Hooyah.

Golden Retrievers

We have more than a few.

I used to be a one dog guy.

I remember my buddy Curtis, black lab mix.

We ran everywhere together.

If I hit the water he never left my side.

Never on a leash.

He was my "swim buddy"... In SEAL Speak that is special. I used to leave him out all day on a wire run when I was at work.

He's gone. I keep his collar behind my seat in the car. He looked away when I was driving him to the vet.

Now we have Goldens and some others. They are our everyday family. It is those eyes. Never violate those eyes. Look at the innocence that remains constant as they age. Look at the unconditional love that is shared. It is as amazing as the cosmos. A miracle when you think about it.

But oh..., we take so much for granted. They don't. They are dogs. Unlike them, we are beginning to believe that we are owed something.

"If I hit the water he never left my side."

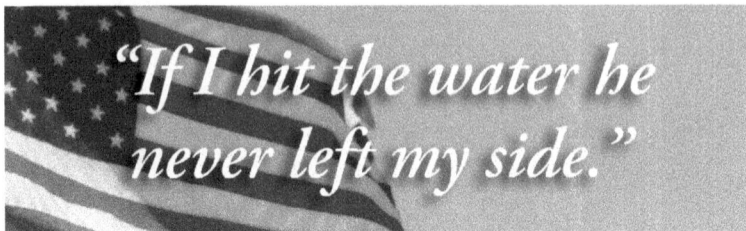

Notice how much complaining there is about my rights this and my rights that?

Goldens are so pretty. What a color!… and no hours at the hair salon! They live from meal to meal. From hug to pat to hug again. They have to wait to be let out, and have to keep their paws crossed hoping they will go on a walk with you.

Wouldn't it be great to be a Golden? Everything would be so simple. Lift a leg, that's all.

But… and this is the big but. They can't do anything about abuse or hunger. They can bark, but not talk… not express their feelings. No sir, most dogs live scary lives in silence.

Not us. We have feelings and we have mouths. We sure make sure that everyone knows them both. Feelings are driving everything these days. They are speeding through stop signs. And no tickets are being issued.

Stop signs are actually being taken down as they are a nuisance. Right wing ideology. Moral values that aren't digital. Antiquated. Interference to progress.

Getting a driver's license is easier than ever.

Don't want to hurt any feelings.

We don't want to tell anyone they are doing something wrong.

Judging is a sign of weakness.

Except it has never been worse.

If I could only bark louder.

Hooyah.

Forever Silent

What do we know about what we don't know about?

How can we judge when we don't know the whole Truth?

But we do judge, and fervently claim we are right.

Do we have heroes we never know about?

The submariner's Silent Service?

The CIA operative?

The Green Beret alone out there?

The Stealth flight that never existed?

The SEAL returning unseen?

The private pain of a veteran?

The tear of a wife?

Heroes in humility.

Keeping us free.

Allowing us to smile.

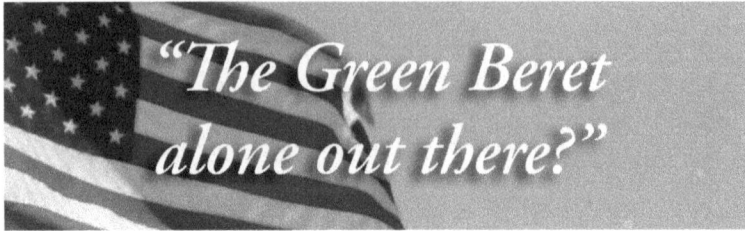
"The Green Beret alone out there?"

Who pins the medals on them?

We will never know.

They want it that way.

God Bless America.

Hooyah.

Black Hole

I can't see the bottom!

How deep is it?

How far down do I have to go?

Can I take a light with me?

It is so dark and scary.

You go first.

Is it in a cave? Or on the ocean floor where it is dark already. Is it in a mine or is it below a large grating underground? If it just wasn't so black down there….

In outer space are the largest black holes of all where scientists say there is nothing. Yet those black holes consume galaxies and stars. Creating a black density that defies logic. Well… at least street logic.

In either case, what is unimaginable is horrific. Where nothing exists?

Actually, black is made up of all colors. We all become one color? Maybe black?

So what is all the fuss? Let's take color out of the equation and let's take

"I can't see the bottom!"

religion out, and let's take histories out. Oh, and lastly, let's just take labels out... Of our clothes too.

Let's just be people. Good and bad.

The good people can fight the bad. Let's hope the former win.

I'd rather be with the good people. What does it take to join? Are there more good people than bad? Usually numbers matter.....

I hear that most quit trying to be a good person worthy of the Good People Army, GPA.

The secret is to be a good person day by day, one day at a time... just giving it all to your instructors who you have to trust. Like in Hell Week in the SEALs... Life was never meant to be easy...

Look around and under the surface of all you know. There are some tough struggles going on. Children who are lost in attitude. Adults unhappy with income, station, or relationships..... So caught up in self that they can't become truly good.

Truly good means thinking of others first. Getting out of yourself makes you gooder.

You are in a black hole until then.....

To get to the outer reaches of the universe it takes a long time with even the best spacecraft... if ever.

But we all gotta try.

Not the Orion, but the USS Faith.

Never quit and black will be white.

What do you think Wayne??

Hooyah.

Bang Bang

BANG BANG, you almost shot me down.

Great song by a great singer during great times, the 60's.

Our society was in transition on so many fronts.

Looking back now it was a period so rich in music from the Beatles to Beach Boys to Sonny & Cher… the list is endless.

The world was in turmoil with the war in Vietnam. Lapels and pants for men were narrow (and it is headed back there today). It seems like a miracle that we have survived all that has transpired since then, much less since WWII.

Miracle is a word that suggests some amazing, almost impossible feat. It is a word that we use when we describe when something really fortuitous, something really good happens to someone. "It must be a miracle that Vickie was not killed by the car that ran the red light". You know what I mean. Or "It was a miracle I made it back from Afghanistan alive." Or "It was a miracle that Sally's baby survived…"

Miracles? Science is a miracle. Can we believe the mathematics that works from science? Or physics or chemistry or medicine? Think about all the things that you can characterize as a "miracle." I think we all have

used the word to describe something that cannot be explained. Usually a miracle is something good.

Have we ever heard someone say that a murder or a disaster was a miracle? I really feel that the birth of a child is a miracle to behold. In fact, most of us marvel at the birth of most anything... puppies, kittens, calves, foals... and on and on. Why is it that we cherish and marvel at that moment?

Is there not something so special and miraculous about it? A birth is a gift to life.

We cradle, caress, protect and love anything just born. The most special of all things we experience while alive on planet Earth.

Planet Earth is a miracle of sorts. I had the blessing to play a small part in our space program. Man flung man into orbit in Gemini and Apollo spacecraft where they took the most amazing pictures of planet Earth. Look how dead the moon is. Look how alive Earth is. The blue of the oceans, the white of the weather, the brown and green of the land. Amazing. What a miracle.

Well... science and mathematics got our astronauts back safely to Earth (...with a little help from my buddies.) There was joy on the carrier; there was joy in the nation. Akin to the joy of birth or the saving of a life. You know, let's look at joy for a moment. Is it not the very best of feelings? Where does it come from? It is a miracle in its own right that joy is part of the mix of existence.

Look how far man has come in the last 2,000 years AD.

Look how far man has grown in the last 10,000 years. Well… except that he has not lost his penchant for war, lust, greed, evil, and self-centeredness…

That aside, it is amazing. Just think that the ignorant fire starter caveman now holds an iPad!! Miracle?

What I like better is that he evolved from some ape animal which evolved from some simple cell form of life which happened when some live dust particles from a billion light years away created our solar system.

What I like best of all with this whole interpretation of our miraculous existence is that it all started with a bang, a really big bang. Miracle.

That explains it all.

But I just don't accept it.

There had to be a bang bang — a First Bang before the big bang created by Something that had energy and design.

Otherwise nothing makes sense.

Science makes no sense unless there was a bang bang miracle.

Thank God for bangs.

Hooyah.

The Grave

Why does it happen?

Why?

When we are young and vibrant our bodies do anything we ask of them.

You can even become a SEAL.

It seems like life is pain and pleasure, never to end.

Love is sought and consumed.

Truth is elusive and found often too late.

I just learned my golden retriever is dying five minutes ago. That is why I am writing this.

His face and eyes are so vibrant as they penetrate your soul with trust and joy. He is old.

He was our first dog in Maine… Well… he came in a crate from the Midwest on a truck. Certainly symbolic of humble beginnings. He lucked out as he got a great life with some other great dogs and a few great people. Unconditional love… where in the hell can you find it??? In his eyes for sure.

"Goodbye my dear friend."

I was thinking that Heaven might allow us to rejoin with the spiritual essence of our pets and past. Would be nice... I am not talking about Mom and Dad or grandparents... just my dogs.

Gets you in your gut every time anything dies that is loved or appreciated... Here I am thinking about existence... being defined by the grave.

If we all respected death maybe we could better respect life. Today there is little respect for anything. That is why I like the military as it teaches you respect, as do good parents, as do people who have the courage to say NO.

The grave can teach you everything you want to know, because at that time the eulogy is read it details how much the person accomplished, acquired, and enjoyed. Most eulogies are superficial as they talk about the material, not the spiritual essence of the individual.

Details that are important are not checks written, but time given to those who were hurting, to those in need. Were you a person who served the humblest or the mighty?

At the gravesite, where tears water the new sod, is the Truth.

Read the words reflected in the tears and you may find out who you were.

Goodbye my dear friend.

Goodbye Kenne.

May He soon pat you on the head.....

Hooyah.

Blue Prayer

A dot on the blue.

A boat.

A blue line from horizon to horizon.

A white cloud.

Above and below.

Slip into the silence.

Face mask narrowing vision to what is in front of you. Pulling, compelling, awe invoking.

Beauty humbles. Close to heaven.

The world underneath the surface of the blue water becomes a prayer. Corals shaped by the random whimsy of unseen nature.

Colors of new rainbows.

Fish swimming in and out with the freedom humans know not. Iridescent lines of verse. Glorifying Creation.

One gently glides one's fins to explore the next 6 feet, senses heightened to the unexpected. Which is always.

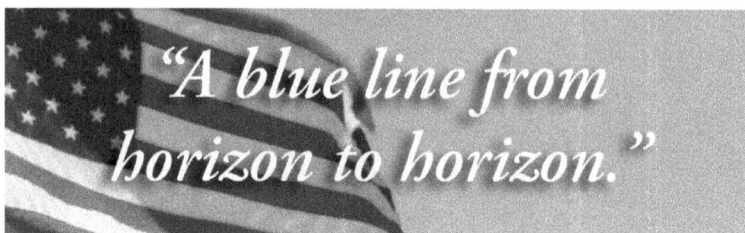
"A blue line from horizon to horizon."

Deeper is darker. Foreboding… yet calling one to dare….

Shallower is brighter… where color explodes. Intensities unseen above. Only in the churches of the oceans.

The only sounds being the parrot fish crunching the coral…. And of course, your bubbles. Your bubbles disturbing the holy serenity.

With skill and new gear no bubbles are near. And silence is again married to silence.

Man floats weightless like in space in liquid. Weightlessness is a cathedral of its own. Except… kneeling is without effort.

Man has just begun to see and map all the beauty. Is not beauty sometimes best left alone? Like the innocence of a child. Who wants to be the first to steal it? No one.

But we do. We swim through life unaware of the stems broken off the coral. Of the people we ignore with an unseen rudeness. With small hurts rendered indifferently.

We take care of ourselves first.

Priority me.

Not Thee...

Find that small boat in the vastness of the blue.

Bobbing in the blue horizon.

Unseen but by the fish below.

And say a prayer.

A blue one.

Hooyah.

Evolution

Can't anyone prove anything?

We are so wound up, liberal and conservative, with issues of rights and interpretations and political correctness that we are self-destructing in a mush of counter-counter-accusations.

Are we evolving into intellectual extinction???

It used to be that we believed in our cornerstones. Our emigrant forefathers came here with solid dreams and beliefs. They adjusted to the English language and the porridge of cultures that became America. They fought rotten wars with courage and pride. They gave up limbs and psyche to protect our way of life… And our Constitution.

Where are we? Has sacrifice been in vain? Where are we going? Tell me!!! Someone tell me!!! No. More importantly, where did we come from??? Where???

The atheist believes in evolution and science can take us back thousands of years. It is fascinating stuff and our DNA appears to be rich with all kinds of primate and sub-primate ancestors. (I know, I have often been accused of thinking like a monkey by my wife… and we won't quote the other things she has compared me to…)

OK, and when the astronomers look deep into the heavens at the current record holder for farthest galaxy away, MACS0647-JD, a trifle 13.3 billion light-years away, they cannot conclude that this is the last galaxy.

You and I know the odds are that if we got a better telescope the end would never be in sight. So existence seems to go out to infinity and beyond. Go figure? Does that make sense? Balderdash. Of course, this is just this one man's opinion.

Oh, I forgot the Big Bang Theory. That is even more ridiculous. What started that?? The NRA??

The renowned scientist atheists, Keith, Watson, Moore and Epp, said that they just could not prove evolution. Science could not prove ultimate evolution... That that whole rationale was defective, reaching a dead end in supposition. But because they chose not to believe in creation or God, they had no choice but to support evolution.

LOOK AT THESE QUOTES from a SEAL buddy's paper*.

Sir Arthur Keith states, "Evolution is unproved and improvable; we believe it only because the only alternative is special creation which is unthinkable."

Professor D.M.S. Watson expresses, "Evolution itself is accepted by zoologists, not because it has been observed to occur or can be proven by logically coherent evidence, but because the only alternative, special creation, is clearly unthinkable."

Professor T.L. Moore states, "The more one studies paleoanthropology, (the fossil record), the more certain one becomes that evolution is based on faith alone."

Theodore H. Epp remarked that everything we can see exists, but since we refuse to believe in God, we choose to believe that it was brought to existence through evolution. Epp goes on to say that you cannot believe in God, and not give him credit for your creation.

It takes a greater leap of faith to believe in evolution than it does in God. Mock me all you want. Bring it on. Love it.

How in the world has the Bible helped so many for so long? How do its words resonate so clearly from some pretty rough and uneducated guys 2,000 years ago? That makes no sense unless it does. What is wrong with right? What is good about evil?

The Bible may be stories to the atheist, to the cynic, but to beautiful people I know it is a tool for clarity and purpose, for humility and unselfishness, for giving and not taking, for serving and not being served. Lives have been saved by Faith, lives have been turned around by Faith, even death has been ennobled by Faith.

I cannot see galaxies, but I can see need.

And we need God.

Creation is all that makes sense.

Hooyah.

* Quotes taken from the paper: Creation/Evolution (THE BURIED TRUTHS), by Rey Ruidiaz

We the Free

Surrounded by ocean.

We are set free from the worries of tyranny.

Few have a clue of what we had to do.

To create this paradise for you and for me.

Guns sounded.

Sailors "drownded".

In wars across the sea… for we the free.

Our borders are water.

Sometimes it is healthy to put on the other shoe.

Try someone else's to see how it fits and feels.

Suppose your neighbor just wanted to kill you.

And the border is just a line in the sand?

Oh, to be free of that chance.

"Sailors 'drownded'."

But we are don't you see?

We are not Israel.

It is just you and me.

Would you die to be free?

Hooyah.

ROE

Where do fish come from that are not fried?

Eggs, dummy.

Egg clusters that make caviar.

It is funny that all fish come from little round gooey things.

Kinda like where we get our beginnings. Mom knows.

Mom raised us all by making sure we did only the right things that she knew.

Well, from her parents eggs… LOL

The first things we really remember about our moms are love and rules. She knew life and her role was to protect and nurture.

Our dads are the same but they have stricter rules… or should have.

Boys and girls need to be forged. I worry that the forging process these days is being diluted by political correctness and other shifts in cultures.

Social networks tend to be rule free.

Think about it.

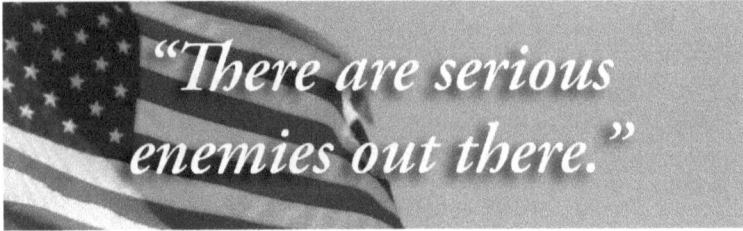
"There are serious enemies out there."

No rules???

When we get engaged there are rules of behavior so the wedding comes off as it should. With both families feeling proud. So the values of the past may have a shot at survival.

Today rules have become political footballs. Fine print infests all rules. So you can't really figure out what a rule is other than from the latest litigation.

There are serious enemies out there. They must be identified and disposed of. Life is not about social networking. There will be no social networking if the current evils are allowed to grow unchecked. Hello?

ROE. Rules of Engagement have been challenging the soldier for decades. We worry so much about unjust collateral damage that the bad guy is given refuge in our ROE. Bureaucracy is redefining inefficiency and inaction. The special operations warrior has his box rebuilt daily. It is a miracle they don't explode. But they don't. That is who they are.

Get the politicians out of war. Get their fingers off the triggers. The focus group is ambushing our advantage.

Where have all the good rules gone?

Moralities abandoned.

Values lost.

Enemy dis-engaged.

Hooyah

Angelfish

What does an angel look like?

Have you known one?

Or are they just winged figures on the ceilings of the Vatican?

So many angels are never seen....

Maybe because we don't want to or just don't believe in what is not on Facebook....

If you slide into the blue water beneath your boat over a coral reef somewhere you come across an amazingly flat graceful angel. Not edible, just beautiful. What a blessing to see one, to see that their uniqueness was created somehow. Somehow?

Tiny ones can be found in aquariums, delighting the eyes of children. Very large ones in oceans everywhere. "Mommy, are angels fish?"

Like in life you have to fish for angels. You have to know where to look. Under the surface. Wherein sings a soul existing for others.

Angels are everywhere

Open your eyes and believe.

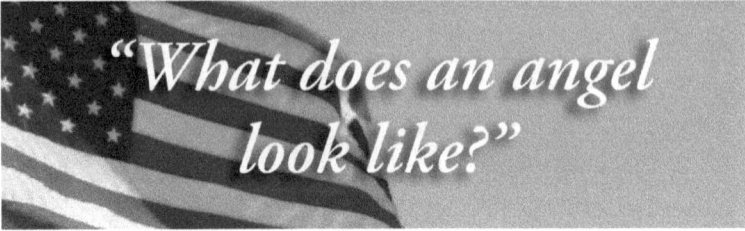

"What does an angel look like?"

And say a prayer.

A blue one.

Hooyah.

Only Easy

At BUDS there is an expression; "The only easy day was yesterday."

It's really about life, marriage, work, family, and fighting for what has value.

What that is, is for us to decide.

But if there is nothing you will fight for, then you are nothing.

When you are young and strong little seems impossible. If you are in Hell Week and cold, nothing is probable. The moment must be seized with resolve, humor, cursing, and caring. You won't quit if your concern is the men around you… your new brothers in pain. One exhausting hour after another becomes an investment in the future. An investment in making it to Friday. Each hour is an accomplishment to be proud of. You build on it and feed from it.

Don't quit on your family and they will know not to quit on you. Once yesterday is yesterday the pain is just a passing event. It no longer hurts. It was easy.

Today, in the moment, is the challenge. Attitude shapes all. Blood is a badge. A smile from your misery mate is a badge. Smiles affirm pride, the right kind. The heads lower and you get on with the next evolution.

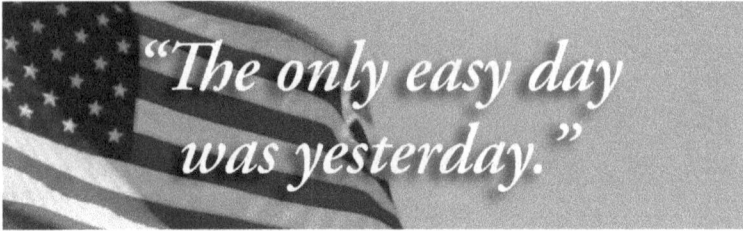

"*The only easy day was yesterday.*"

No cell phones to get assurance from. Too bad and too late. Your only phone is your smile.

Isn't a smile so fantastic when you catch one from a person under great stress? Coping by seeing some humor in a desperate moment.

"The only easy day was yesterday." bonds thousands of guys who know what it means. It is worth it to find out what it means first hand.

You just have to know how to run and swim easily. Do not wait until the last minute or the last year. Learn about the ocean…. Surf…. Learn how to fire a gun… go out in the woods and get lost….. and figure it out.

Don't be easy on yourself.

Life isn't easy.

The unexpected is to be expected.

Be proud of yesterday.

Make today a great yesterday too.

And… keep the Faith.

Hooyah.

First Family

I know two women who had no idea of what they were getting into.

Just for fun I will spell their names backward to protect their identities, Aim and Nitsirk. *(They are now in charge of marketing this book.)*

This is not about the White House, so all you politico thrill seekers can relax.

This is about a place that is much more stressed and much more valuable.

This is about what the White House is supposed to be made of.

It is about the blood and values of the American family. Everyone in the military is part of the fiber of freedom. For freedom ceases to exist when what we hold important is diluted and squandered.

Sometimes debate is too late. Without a military you can't debate. No threat, no attention.

Every man who goes into the military learns much more about life than he would as a civilian in those young years …. Mostly wandering… philosophically….

Rules, regulations, integrity, trust, honesty… and the meaning of the

"Aim and Nitsirk"

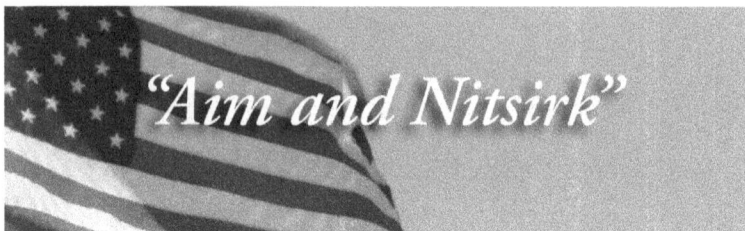

word "NO" penetrate his being. 18-20 year olds from WWII to Korea to Vietnam to Iraq to Afghanistan and beyond get sobered up to the realities of the world and the uniqueness of our democracy.

I strongly believe in a universal draft like they have in Israel. Then all men will be bonded in a strong and personal way and have the basic skills for whenever....

To make us strong, they have to be strong... and for them to be strong their family must be strong. And that cannot happen if their family does not come first. The wife and mother of their family has to do all the work a husband usually does and then theirs too. From the beds, the home, the schools, the lawn, the bills, the worry.... their days are more than full. There is never any time off to drink beer and watch TV.

No, their lives are not on the line... but if the soldier does not come home.... Their lives are lost. Or if he comes home injured their lives are upside down from whatever dreams they had.

So the First Family is your family, is our family, and our country's family.

It is a tough new environment with social networking, texting, Skype, and the rest. Contact is available but also not realistic for the battle front.

I don't have the answer.

But you can pray together.

I can't imagine praying with my kids via Skype when I am heading out into the dark unknown to find an enemy who is hiding and waiting.

Hooyah.

Morale Compass

You have to keep the spirits up.

Inside you first, then your men, and your family.

You can't do your job without your spirits in the right place.

A little trash humor never hurt if the timing was precise.

Otherwise, just do something for anyone else and they will be lifted, as will you.

Without morale you can't fight or communicate as a unit. As with your family you can't love as a unit if moms, dads, or the kids, or wifey, or girlfriend aren't in good spirits.

Tricky terrain these feelings…. Takes a lot of training too. Trial by fire in the emotional shoot house of life. Anything can go wrong there too…

Everything has to be in order to have a perfect mission. Everything.

The right directions have to be offered. The GPS points have to be precise. Caution must be intelligent. True North must be exact.

The best path is one that takes you to a safe and a good place. This can only be where good is good and bad is bad. Plain and simple. You can't get there without values… and damn good ones. Not half-ass excuses for values.

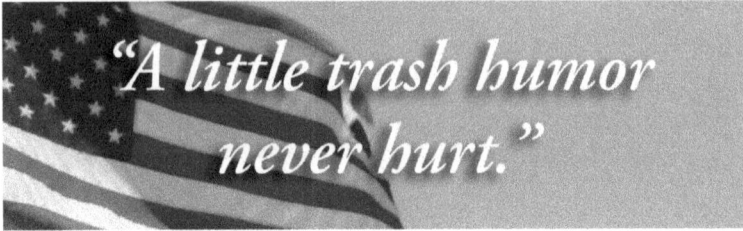

> "A little trash humor never hurt."

We are all fighting for values. For what is valuable. Again I say… for family, for friends, for country, and for freedom. You can't win this battle without morals.

Hello? Morals define values. It is harder to be moral that to do the O-Course with a broken wrist. But not quitting on this goal is worth every day of pain, discipline, and fortitude.

Moral compass my friends. Moral compass. You set your own True North. You define it. Listen to your heart. Look family in the eyes and see the reflection of your Truth in their faces. Look for the twitch that says you aren't there yet.

Without a moral compass we are lemmings in the sea of self.

Without a moral compass we are just swarms of look-a-likes….

Field Manual 101 is the Bible.

It ain't an easy read.

But neither was BUDS.

Hooyah.

Valuables Protection

Protect your valuables.

Should be the trademark for Jockey shorts, eh?

You know the specific pain when your valuables get hurt.

The world stands still, so to speak.

Your buddies laugh.

You are so bent over you can't give them the finger.

We are willing to fight for our valuables. What is a valuable? It is something that has value. In this case, real value…

But beyond that are the values of freedom, Truth, family, fairness, and many more. Take them away and there is nothing.

We have problems today. Values have no value unless they are a law.

Everything that we have held dear has been under attack by legal interpretations and lawsuits. If you voice your opinion on anything you believe in public and social media, everyone who disagrees is on the attack. And it can be hurtful. So we are starting to hide our values. We are starting to lose.

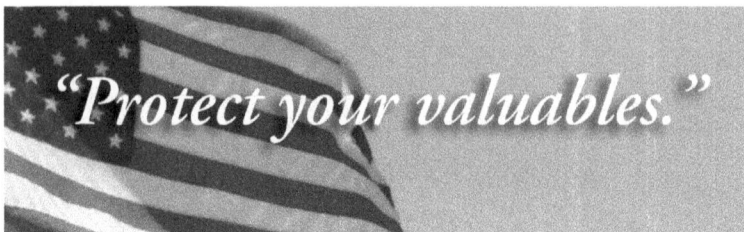
"Protect your valuables."

Local, state, and national governments are asked to create more and more laws to fine tune perceived fairness until it is not fair. It is not only not fair, but it has become stupid.

How in the world do we protect our valuables?

Heaven only knows what will happen with the chaos in the Middle East. Talk about an assault on and a desecration of values… Our new laws mean nothing at a beheading.

Who is going to say "NO" I cannot stand it anymore?

Should lawyers pack? It is a legal war on values.

Now we call them old-fashioned values. I guess labeling them "old" neutralizes them.

Head-in-the-sand no longer cuts it.

We can send our military to weird places to do their work, but who is going to do it at home? Clergy can't do any more than they are.

When will each one of us speak up?

Who will teach our children about respect, honesty, Truth, and love?

"NO" must be "No" again.

When did we become so afraid of saying it?

Where have all the fathers gone?

Who is going to protect our valuables?

Ouch!

Hooyah.

Beyond the Pews

What the heck in the world is a pew?

I just checked Wikipedia and it says something to do with long wooden benches in churches with aisles so you can get in and out fast.

Then is it "pew" or "phew"?

I know many assume the latter.

Either way the world tends to avoid both.

You know, nobody wants to be told anything by anybody. Each individual prefers to chart their own course without advice… They don't want advice, they don't need it. And the younger you are the more you complain and "attitude out" when an opinion is offered, especially from anyone older.

Ironic, ain't it??? You try to help someone and often your intent is twisted into an offense and walls of feelings arise. "You are hurting me" is the message. Oh well, so what else is new??? We are becoming a culture which is afraid to hurt feelings, so inaction rules. Oh well…

But back to the pews… the non-smelly kind…

Pews conjure up the image of sitting in a church with everyone looking at you… and you are supposed to know all about God… I can't imagine

"Then is it 'pew' or 'phew'?"

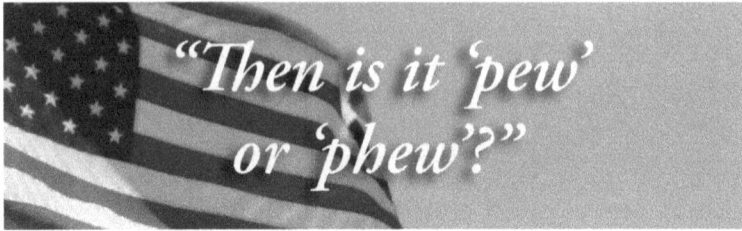

anything more unpleasant!!! Waterboarding begins to sound nice… Well, this is how many feel who don't even open a church door, much less the many who are inside… and then sit as far back as possible to avoid judging eyes and take easy exits… Maybe everybody in church should wear sunglasses???

Now, you know what you get in pews??? Pulpit ADVICE… lots of it from the living and the dead. Advice is everywhere. A maelstrom of advice… and they say it is all from God!!! OMG get me out of here… Talk about a marketing nightmare? Make people want to come to church? There is no ad firm willing to take it on. There are so many church haters out there that I keep my opinion to myself… mention church at a cocktail party and you would think you were a serial killer.

They say religion has made a mess of the world. Hey "they"… go back to where you came from. Hidden in religion are values offering the only way out of slavery to self and bigotry.

Lost in church histories of shame and hypocrisy are the heroic examples of truth, love, and selflessness. Powerful stories bringing all to their knees in awe. There is enormous good and it is amazing.

A young child senses good and speaks to it, often amazing us. The idealism of youth bespeaks of truth and good. We still revere character, perseverance, and humility. These stories can rarely be found in the media, but in church they abound in overwhelming poignancy and frequency.

Kind of like "seek and ye shall find." The thing is that it requires effort to find out the Truth. Spiritual inquisitiveness is not effort free.

We have the courage to climb Mt. Everest without oxygen. But we don't have the courage to enter a church with an open mind.

Take the beautiful Olympics which are testimony to achievement on the purest of scales. No one cheats to get the gold, there is no easy way. Real dedication, sacrifice of time and self to be tested in that one final moment. If you win, it was worthwhile. If you lose it can be worthwhile. Discipline and values. Reward lies therein.

If you want to become a Navy SEAL you have to give all you have and more. You are allowed and even encouraged to quit at any moment. Is the achievement worth the pain?

To be a good, really good human is the price worth the effort?

It means giving up most everything, especially the desires of the self.

Because to be a really good human you have to care about others more than you care about yourself.

This is an insurmountable obstacle for many. Why?

Really good human beings are just regular people who didn't quit…

Don't sell yourself short…

Try Church.

God Bless You.

Hooyah.

Sameless

Shameless the way some people behave.

You just want to look away sometimes.

But maybe we are looking away more and more today.

Shameless.

The headlines reek of inevitable war. Of unspeakable acts going on every day. I don't get it. Why do people still hold human life so inconsequential? Is it centuries of poverty and lack of leadership? Is a religion all that gives hope?

Is not atrocity unacceptable? Women and even children? Hello world?

Text bombs don't appear to be stopping anything but good.

Shameful.

At what point or border do our brothers cease being our brothers?

What if we didn't fund Special Operations? Those guys go where none of us wishes to go. They get sent because it means fewer lives to risk rather than the thousands with the forces actually required. We pat them on the back and have no clue what they do. Do for us, that is. Shameful.

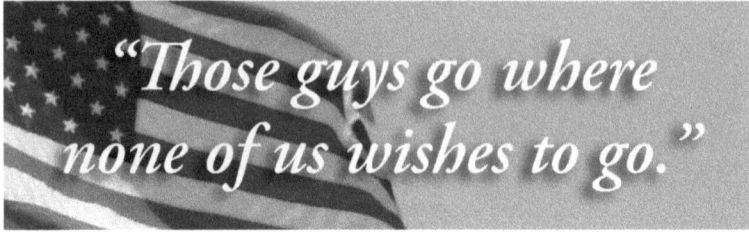

"Those guys go where none of us wishes to go."

They can only be successful in cloaks of total secrecy. We are doing our best to take that away from them. Shameful. Shameless.

Evil so sublime is also infiltrating our culture. It seems like we are being called to sameness. Every special interest is claiming foul and unfairness so law after law is being enacted. The majority is becoming overwhelmed by the minority's claims.

See the parallel between the Middle East and our "Sames"? We are fighting politically to all have the same opinions. Are we beheading values? Law after law calling us to act and think the same. Really good people are afraid to speak up for fear of being drowned out by the placard people.

"Sameless" is now a word that defines this new war. Do we want to allow ourselves to be more or less the same? Look-a-Likes?

Maybe we need some moral SEALs to take on the fight when they are discharged.

Who else can we turn to?

Google: SEALs For Christ…

Hooyah.

Eyes On

"There they are."

"Adjusting the windage."

"Are you sure?"

"Send it."

Sometimes decisions just have to be made. Every adjustment to clarify the Truth is essential. What more can you do? Not to face evil with immediate resolve risks death of the more innocent.

There are moral moments where an immediate decision is necessary. But the allure of pleasure clouds the process and the windage cannot be set and the target of safety is missed. We go through life seeking the pleasure of acceptance and material comfort and sensual sojourns…. Only to find we have missed the target, our own self-fulfillment.

Read the papers where so many celebrities and wealthy and poor are unhappy when they reach their later years….. Fake smiles and tales of happiness hide their Truths. For happiness only comes when you help someone else. Try it. It is seductive too.

The eyes have it.

"Adjusting the windage.

Most everything is brought to us first through our eyes.

Eyeglass frame designs are in the millions. All to make your eyes look fashionably better and to see better. Transition lenses, trifocal, mirrored, sport.... Designers are making fortunes just off designing frames with their names on them. On your eyes!!!

Optometrists are working overtime to help us see.

I sure love what my eyes can see. When I was young it was all about activities and pleasure.

Then I started to see with my heart and things changed, really changed... I could see how happy people were, but also how sad. I can see subtle pain with the slightest glance.

Opportunities to reach out and reassure are now in abundance.

Amazing. Amazing. All around me. I never knew it was there all the time.

It hurts seeing other's pain.

But it is an honor.

It humbles one.

But there is no time to waste.

There is no time to hesitate.

"Send it."

Hooyah.

Hurry Up

Who says it first in your family?

Hurry up dear!

Now I know we guys don't like to be told to hurry up.

I assume all women expect it as they have so much stuff to organize…

How about teens? Are they ever ready? Are they ever on time??

Ever going on a trip and have your wife tell you to hurry up packing when she is telling you what to pack???

In the military everything is hurry up and wait. OMG at Ft. Benning we must have laid under trees for shade for a day in oppressive heat for a flight. Rush, rush, rush. Wait.

In life things seldom go as planned. But plans there must be as lives are at stake.

Actually having to wait can insure all ground is covered and last details re-sorted out.

Making kids wait is one of the best things you can do and teach. Wait for waiting's sake and wait for a purpose. Both are important. Teach them. On space launches there are built-in waits.

Wait until the Seeing Eye Dog is fully trained? Wait until the broken leg heals?

Wait until the heart mends and feelings are back to normal. It is hard to wait, but it can be done with dignity and humor.

But the biggest wait in life is putting off what one calls "religion". "Religion" has become a bad word these days. Who wants to be associated with such a criticized position? So Christianity is almost being forced underground…. To wait???

No, to regroup, and find its correct path and then, after the wait, stand tall and sublimely obvious.

But this wait is not really about organized denominational religion. It is about what you feel deep inside about right and wrong. The journey to God is within. His Holy Spirit abides in each of us. It was there from birth. Look back at your first sense of fairness…..

We allow ourselves to allow the walls of hypocrisy, ignorance, insecurity, and denomination to rule our judgments. These walls give us superficial excuses to wait and put off serious reflection about God.

But when that time comes… and….

If you don't ever quit on Jesus…

Then you will find out who you were really meant to be.

Don't wait any longer.

Hooyah.

Chicken Neck

Do you remember back when you were young and others dared you to do something?

Or when you dared someone?

Immediately, if there was hesitation… the label "chicken" was thrown on the emotional table.

Nope, no one ever wants to be called a "chicken". Especially SEALs…. LOL

Well, Marines too, and all the rest.

I guess I can't call a base jumper "chicken". Jumping off mountains to free fall…. Or even Astronauts. Or even Pastors taking on the cynics…. Nope… no chickens there… Or even mothers raising children, much less doing it alone….

I remember an afternoon after Hell Week when we were taken to the woods to camp out before doing an overnight demolition raid on a bridge 10 miles away. We had to arrive at dawn unseen to position our dummy charges. No clue what the night would bring, stumbling with precision through the black wilderness.

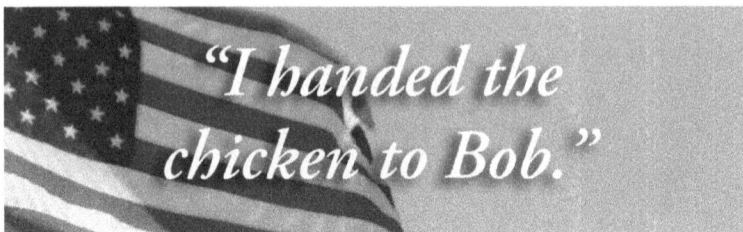

We were each given a shelter half (Aka half a tent). So my tent buddy and I put it together and prepared to get some sleep. But dinner first. We were hungry. (You are hungry all the time during Hell Week training) We had a pot of water, some potatoes and… were given a live chicken. My sense of humor kicked in and I quickly gave her a name and started petting her, like a golden retriever.

Now… I had no farm experience. I did not know my tent mate's background. Well, it became the time to de-feather and boil the chicken, but …. it had to be killed first…. Seizing the moment I handed the chicken to Bob for the ceremony. To my surprise, he declined to kill it. I had no clue what I was doing, but with a big smile I grabbed it and twisted its neck off.

That was the last thing I ever killed. He went on to Vietnam and also became a Commanding Officer of SEAL Team 6.

I left the Navy after 4 years and in one month went from "high explosives to handbags".

Our paths diverged so incredibly.

I have no clue of the covert activities he managed in his career.

But I do remember that moment when a chicken neck was going to link us forever.

Life gives us all unique moments that are ours alone.

Cherish them.

They must be gifts from Somewhere?

Hooyah.

No Buds

Today is Memorial Day 2015.

I took a half hour walk this morning.

I used to run but heart surgery has changed my lifestyle.

I have run thousands of miles in my lifetime.

From Europe to China. The first plane into Beijing and Shanghai after normalization in 1975. Runs in smoke, cold, and fog… Alone for miles. No one would look up. They were scared of westerners and didn't want to get in trouble.

The sounds of the people at exercise or work was its own symphony. All around the world. Birds. Running was a journey into the vibrancy of the unknown.

Real entertainment. Not a reality show.

Recently I have been trying out some wireless ear buds. I have noticed all the young wearing them all the time be it for phone or music. Exercise machines are driven by their drivers who are lost in the music. The outside world is irrelevant. The sounds of the world around are put in their proper place, the background.

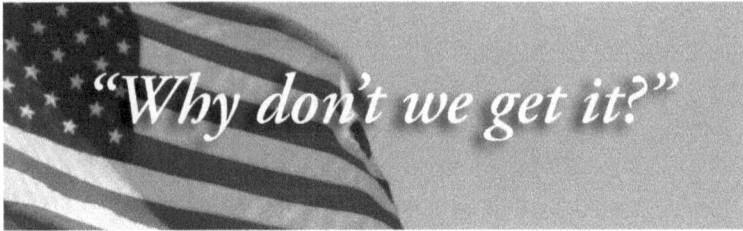

"Why don't we get it?"

These buds are the seeds of pleasure and deceit. The Truth of the moment is obscured by the allure of good music. Reality controlled. The pain of exercise is muted in the distractions of the top 10.

Our world is upside down. It is becoming more and more difficult to deal with our political indecision and with the evil brewing elsewhere.... Certainly in the Middle-East...

A choice is imminent. Tune out... or tune in. Remove the ear buds if you want a shot at surviving.

There are no ear buds at BUD/S.

The harsh reality of unrelenting excessive physical exercise and meaningless repetitions of pain are without the soothing music in the ear... LOL....

If you want to survive and get the prize then your new tunes are the instructor's incessant shouts of criticism. Real music in real time. Molding real musicians with new real instruments, those of war... and our survival.

Why don't we get it?

We argue, criticize, and litigate with so much energy that we are mentally exhausted.

If we don't take the damn things out of our ears there will be no home to come home to.

Why don't we get it?

If we can't hear the Truth…

It will be too late.

No BUDS at BUD/S.

Get it?

Hooyah.

Halo

HALO

High Altitude Low Opening.

It takes Oxygen first, then courage, then training, then a plane, then a cause.

Gotta have them all to be that stupid… at least to the earthbound.

Then you can add weapons, or explosives, or a rebreather and fins.

And then…. fingers that can still cross.

You jump out high… no…forget it…at high altitude…

Track miles to target area… Open low unseen. On land or sea.

No one knows you are there.

Your intel was True.

You get home safe.

When you leave your mother's womb she does her best to give you the courage and skills to navigate life. You start out with her love. Her values, her Truth. The highest preparation.

"Have a Lovely Opening."

However, most all choose to descend to uncharted depths. Where vanity, pride, and insecurity lie.

Mom is gone. The mother ship.

Dad had provided warnings but is often sadly gone when his stern discipline was called for. His Truth not learned.

So many open too low. They can be found regrouping in homeless and addiction centers… if still alive… Rehabilitating because they jumped before they were ready.

To navigate life requires certain wisdoms. The compass is Truth.
It is not sold in a store. Some find it in church. It can always be found in helping others.

Values that have stood the test of time are available at the Jump School in the clouds. If you don't graduate, you jump stupid.

And someone will say that was a dumb-ass thing for you to do.

Maybe old people have landed safely.

Sit down next to one and find out.

You won't be a "dumb-ass".

You get home safe.

Have A Lovely Opening.

"Stand in the door".

Hooyah.

Charity

"To be or not to be?" is a question all charities have to ask themselves.

Their vision is pure.

The execution is treacherous.

One cannot give now without boundaries and rules and scrutiny and judgments and liabilities.

Wow! What if you just want to give?

If your charity starts from genuine Christian compassion you are history. Adios purity, hola political correctness. Want to pray with your clients? Forget it. Want to have Christian symbols on your walls? Forget it… and forget any available government assistance.

Why is a religious affiliation such a problem for us these days? Why do other non- profits have to pretend to be non-Christian to receive government assistance?

This is upside down nonsense. No prayer in schools? How stupid. What are we afraid of that our forefathers weren't?

Bigotry cloaked in "correctness." Christianity has endured 2,000 years of self- inflicted wounds and glory. Why is it the bad guy? We espouse

"What if you just want to give?"

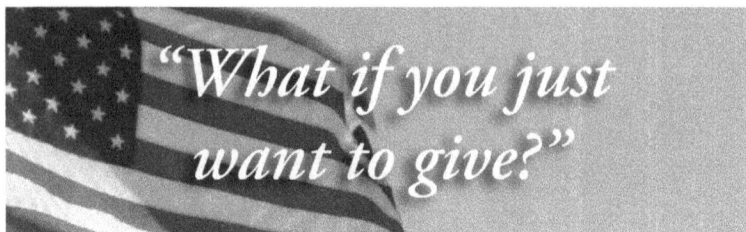

tolerance on so many fronts. We are liberated with our freedoms to protect every sensitivity and every cause. Women's rights, children's rights, bills of rights. I bet you could have "One-Eyed Parrot's Rights"... open up a charity and get federal funding... But if the parrot is a Christian??? Forget it.

Christians these days are intimidated and silent with all the noise going on in the media... much less the stirrings and proclamations in the Middle East. Is it best to be an atheist? Or certainly never share your spiritual leanings out loud in the daytime? I bet a proclaimed atheist will find his own discomfort in Tehran if he doesn't kneel to theirs...

Terrorism is proclaiming "Believe what we do or die!" Your children and families are insignificant to the suicide bomber. OK America, quibble with the funding protocols of charity. Dither in absurdity when your energies should be in strengthening national values and resolve. Unity in compassionate vision with fierce resolve to deny injustice must be carved out of the political quagmire.

Leadership requires clear values, not ones that need to be interpreted in 2,000 pages of legalese. Where did we lose our common sense? Things don't get done unless you do it. That is why I love Nike. "Just do it." That is why the Navy SEALs are so good. Think about it.

What is wrong with "The Pledge of Allegiance"?

Let's be proud of our Christianity again.

There is simply nothing wrong with it.

Jesus was not a bad guy.

Millions can attest that they would not have survived without Him.

Can't we all get along before it is too late?

Hooyah.

LCSR

I bet no one knows the thing ever existed.

It was fast before its time.

Before fast boats ever existed.

It was created back in the early '60s for a special purpose and a special group of guys…. us.

How cool is that?

I am talking twin 1000 HP gas turbine engines driving a 52 foot all fiberglass boat that screamed "do you dare?"…. or "try me and you'll never leave…"

Landing Craft Swimmer Recovery.

She was designed to pick up demolition and reconnaissance swimmers at high speed. It worked. Crazy amazing. Called the Fulton Recovery System and is still used today for covert airplane pickups…

There was a prow hook in the water on the bow that would winch a snagged line in. The boat would approach the center of a line (rope) perpendicular to the two awash sleds with swimmers, and reel them in not slowing down. The sleds would merge behind the stern and be pulled onto a rubber mat that the swimmers could just step onto and

"It was fast before its time."

enter the stern door relatively unseen from the shore because of the high wake. Swimmers could also exit via the rubber mat, jumping into the low center of the wake and not be seen... cool? Sorry, no time to explain it better.

I missed a chance to go to Virgin Gorda on it. I was so young I could not appreciate how amazing it was for its time. It certainly was the precursor for the SEALs amazing fast boats of today. The LCSR is lost to history.

It is also amazing how much we can forget as time passes.

Major accomplishments, on land, in the sea, in space, and in the family all sadly fade.

Maybe with Google nothing will ever be forgotten again. Maybe.

Except we are still fighting the same old wars.

When will we learn?

My old Great Books and Encyclopedias are dinosaurs.

But the LCSR still screams in my dreams...

Hooyah.

The Weaver

There used to be weavers in every town.

Fabrics of every texture and color.

Rugs galore.

Now you can only see real weaving in counties like India. Still beautiful handmade art if you can find it. Otherwise it is all now computerized and a human never touches it. If you want real texture and quality there is nothing like hand woven to stir the senses.

Some things, to be real, have to take real effort… and real effort by the individual. What is simple is always complex if it is meant to be the best.

There is a simple looking obstacle at BUDS. 10 foot 3 inch diameter bars parallel to the ground about 3-4 feet apart that create an inclined up and down design. You run to it then try to find an efficient coordination to weave your body into, under, and above, and under, and above…. Like human thread. Except that it requires real focus, rhythm, and effort to do it fast enough to pass. SEAL candidates trying to be a needle and thread at the same time. You are alone in your head and body. Once it snowed. You do the obstacle many, many times…

"You get good at the obstacles."

especially during Hell Week.... And after. You get good at the obstacles. You have no choice. No time to text.

You learn that life requires you to weave in and out of complicated situations.

You take the word "No" out of your vocabulary.

"Yes Sir, Instructor Sir."

Good preparation for marriage???

"Yes Dear, Of Course Dear."

Hooyah.

Slide For Life

Water slides are fabulous these days.

They even have them on cruise ships… Go figure.

Kids used to pour water with a hose on the top of a slide in a playground and enjoy the wet ride.

Some big slides got dangerous… but still exciting. Who cares anyway when you are young.

A lot of people want to slide through life. So they throw a little alcohol or drugs on it and push off on the easy downhill ride. Except at the bottom the ladder up has rungs too far apart.

The easy way is always the hardest way. Until you learn that the hardest way is the easiest. We humans try to cut every corner there is. We cut too many moral corners. We try to maneuver around the Truth. Guess where it gets us? Not closer to happiness for sure…

Well, now we are forced to go back to the 'O Course' (Obstacle Course) to learn simple lessons. At the Amphibious Base in Little Creek Virginia and also in Coronado California are the only two Slides-For-Life in existence…

There is this 30-40 foot wood frame tower to climb up…At the top is a

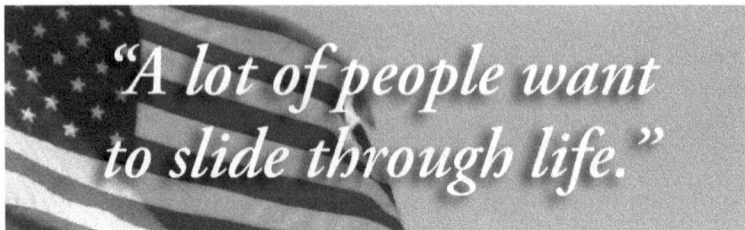

> *"A lot of people want to slide through life."*

ladder to climb to then find a way to jump up at the rope that descends across a water pit for maybe 30 yards. But your body has to be on top of the rope to make any time descending. Let's say it is a leap of Faith to get to where you just start. Hey, it snowed too.

BUDS is all about faith that you won't get killed every time some outrageous task is put forth. Like running up a sand dune backwards…

Life requires all of us to do the impossible at some point.

Faith is required.

Where do you find Faith?

That is what my four hundred 1-800 book chapters are all about.

They are damned good.

Look straight forward, never down, and the Slides-For-Life can be conquered.

Happy guys at the bottom will greet you.

Hooyah.

Round the World

Thank God some bloke discovered the world was round.

Would you believe at one point they thought it was some cube and you could drop off the edge, drown, and cease to exist?

Haven't you ever felt that you were on some dangerous edge? Financially? Emotionally?

We travel all around the world looking at other cultures, their beauty, their history, and their plight. We usually look away from the latter. You learn a lot about life going round the world.

Sometimes our world is right in front of our nose.

For SEALs the world is their responsibility. They never know where they will be sent or if they can ever tell anyone… ever. Their world is black. The night is their domain.

I first heard the phrase "Round The World" on the third day into Hell Week. Sounded like fun. Except for the fact that we would be carrying IBLs, Inflatable Boat Large, on our heads for 24 hours as we paddled on the ocean, on lakes, and maneuvered through woods where we had to carry them on edge to get through the trees. Running, crawling… up

"...on the third day into Hell Week."

sand dunes.... Lots of time for swearing and humor.... You had to be there.... LOL... obstacle course.... Stinky swamp mud..... and even the rock jetty. Did I say it was covered with ice you west coast surfers?? Talk about slippin' and slidin' folks... Shit, it was a masochist's blast.

All is a blur now, but I am sure many quit by Wednesday. We just kept plodding along...and along... try pushups in the sand with the boats on your backs.

The instructors conjured up all kinds of preposterous events that were just to scare us and prompt quitting.

But is not life the same...??

No matter what path you choose there are always curve balls. There are always opportunities to quit.

We have a saying... "Quitting is not an option".... Accepting that, what is one to do??

Keep on keeping on...

One step at a time.

Live in the moment giving it your very best.

It is easier when you are trying to help your struggling buddy, mate, or child.

But just don't quit and you will get round the world.

Now breathe deep, open your eyes, and say "I did it!"

Hooyah.

Big Screw

I bet we all have been screwed at one time.

Something unfair was done to us.

Even robbed of something.

When you gamble you get screwed.

When you play with the Truth you will get screwed.

The big screw is coming.

It's in the Middle East.

My first big screw came in Key West.

We were at Underwater Swimmers School at the Navy Base.

That night, in pairs, we entered the harbor with closed circuit oxygen rebreathers. Our assignment was to attack a moored ship at the dock a mile away. It was dark and spooky. You stay close to your swim buddy. It's nice not to be alone, and much less dangerous.

Suddenly the water swirled violently as a school of Jack erupted around us. After swimming at 10 feet for 20 minutes a quick peek indicted we were way off course and out near the harbor entrance. Took a compass

"The big screw is coming."

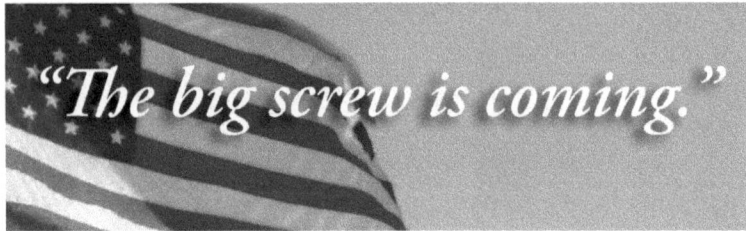

bearing and slipped back below and swam on. Then it felt like we weren't moving. We had literally swum into the fine mud bottom where the silt density changed so slowly we didn't initially notice. Yuck luck.

Came up again for a peek and swam for another 20 minutes until I hit something solid. We were in the pilings under a pier a good 40 yards from our target.

There was one problem. A moored submarine was between us and our target. Perpendicular. What to do? My logic said do not gamble going back out to the harbor but take a direct shot by going under the sub which would allow a straight course to the ship.

We go down, embracing the enormous circumference of the submarine. At her keel point she was only 3 feet off the hard sand bottom. Oops. If she decided to ballast and sink a little deeper we could be pressed into the bottom.

We turned over and put our stomachs to the hull and swam. Then the straight course to our target.

Real dark.

My hands touched and groped on something metal and big. It was a giant propeller, maybe 15 feet wide... We swam the propeller shaft to the hull and placed our dummy mine and rose to the surface with pride and jest to the surprised crew.

Mission accomplished.

Now that was a big screw!

How do we stop the one headed our way???

Hooyah.

Fire In the Hole

Sometimes when camping as a kid you dug a shallow hole to build a fire in.

Maybe the forerunner of today's fire pits??

We see a lot of fire these days…

From forests, to brush, to CVS drugstores, to historical sites in the Middle-East…

Fire is something which consumes without remorse and without following anything but itself.

Sometimes emotions get out of control and rage like fires.

Is there fire in Washington??

Is entitlement a fire?

Is playing with the Truth a fire?

Everybody in the SEALs knows the expression "Fire In The Hole!" It is something uttered just prior to igniting the blasting cap which ignites the detonating cord which then instantly detonates the 1,000 lbs. of C4 in an instant maelstrom of explosive force.

"Is there fire in Washington??"

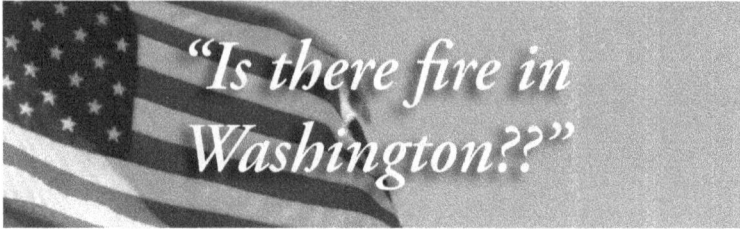

Better keep your heads down.

My swim buddy Bob and I, and our men, had just laid an underwater field off Vieques of 500-1,000 lbs. of C3, and it did not go off. So the two of us, as officers, had the pleasant duty of paddling out over the live field and redoing the fuse assemblies.

When done, I lost the flipped coin and dove down the 10-15 feet and pulled the pins. I think we may have had a 3-5 minute delay built in for us to paddle out of harm's way.

Fire In The Hole!!

As I surfaced, but unexpectedly into the bottom of the IBS (Inflatable Boat Small) rubber raft, I got disoriented and was slow getting aboard and paddling. It all went off. BOOM.... as water flew all around us.

From shore we disappeared in a 200 foot cloud of water. Then smiles from afar as we paddled out of the mist.

Lesson learned.

If one is trained, thinking, and honest, the fires and explosions of life can end the same way.

You will be smarter and more careful.

Especially with the Truth.

PS: When I left the Navy in the summer of '66 I went to work for a department store in NYC on Fifth Avenue, Lord & Taylor. I get to say that in one month I went from High Explosives to Handbags! Yep, as an assistant buyer in the Handbag Department…. In the basement.

Fire In The Hole!

Hooyah.

Running Lights

Would you believe that today joggers go out running at night with small LED flashing lights…. Like giant fireflies?

Men don't run at night with lights. Who ever heard of such a thing? It should be women only… Then you know who to help…LOL wink, wink…

Now cars are mandated to have daytime running lights, DRL. Bright halogen LEDs in every shape that may tell you what kind of car it is…. Crazy times…

Now all you sailors who love the sea cannot go out on your own if you don't know the Rules Of The Road… Or all the nautical traditions that define behavior and right of way at sea.

From sailboats, to motorboats, to yachts, to cruise ships, to freighters, to aircraft carriers… all behave by the same Rules of the Road. At sea everybody has a strict code because if there is an accident you not only get hurt like in a car but you sink too… Much more pride is taken by sailors than drivers….

50 Years ago on a winter night in the Chesapeake, Dan and I had just slipped over the side of our small LCPL boat breathing pure oxygen

"Men don't run at night with lights."

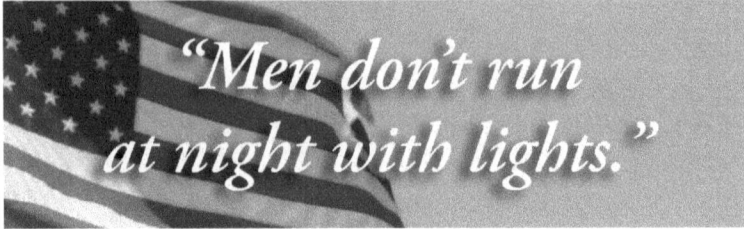

from our Emerson Rebreathers. The target ship was moored about 2 miles away. We took our bearings and started the swim.

After a while I heard this thumping in the black. Thump, thump, thump. We should not have been in the shipping channel. I thought it may be the propeller cavitation of a large ship so I surfaced slowly to take a peek from the top corner of my mask so as not to be seen regardless.

I saw the red and green running lights of a large freighter high off the surface. Running lights are configured so if you only see red then you are looking at her port side. If you only see green, you are on her starboard side. BUT, if you see both she is heading right at you! What to do and to do fast?

I said to Danny, let's go to the bottom at about 50-60 feet and let her pass over. We started down... and would be diving deeper than 33 feet where oxygen becomes toxic. And... also envisioned being involved with the propeller if we erred. I reversed the call and we took off for the surface, figuring we could use the bow wave to separate us from the hull and screws if we were that close. Better to see what is going to happen to you.

She got closer and closer looming above us and... we were spared as she passed within 20 yards to port.

We continued our swim. And smiling, hit our target and rose to the surface with another "Gotcha" for the lookouts who never saw us.

It best to know the Rules of the Road whether at sea or in church.....

Hooyah.

Only Easy

Only easy.

That is the only way losers want to have it.

From poor kids to rich kids…. It is all the same today.

And the keyboard is making everything easier.

Maybe we should send them all to a giant correctional facility in New Orleans, "The Big Easy"… LOL.

The military would not be a bad option. Mandatory draft. I am all for it.

There you learn about not being comfortable, not being able to retreat to your cell phone when upset.

What is wrong with easy anyway? Well… you don't learn a damned thing. Effort is the only teacher. From pain you learn how to avoid it. You learn that the seemingly hard path is really the "Big Easy"…

In the Teams we have this fabulous expression/motto. "The Only Easy Day Was Yesterday." It is over the entrance to the grinder at BUDS in Coronado.

Here is the crucible of doubt and pain. Seemingly endless calisthenics and effort, to dishearten all but the committed. Learning to tune out

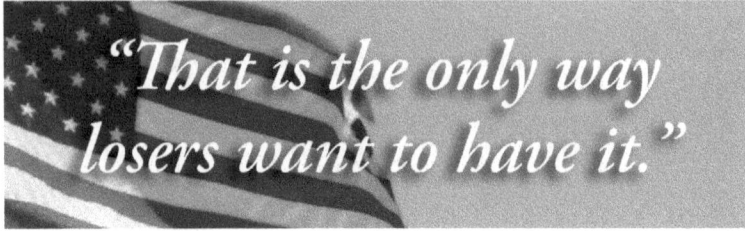

"That is the only way losers want to have it."

and just accept every moment for what it is. That it will pass. That whatever is horrible next can't be known until now is over. Having some pride that you have already accomplished the last hour. This continues to build until you have too much pain invested to quit. The invisible threshold.

Then hours become days. Yesterday always seems easier than today because it wasn't that bad after all if you survived it. Hence the saying.

But this really is a mantra for life.

You want to do good at work?

You want to protect your family?

You want to protect your nation?

You want to protect your heart?

You want to protect your God?

Then embrace every moment.

It could be worse.

"The Only Easy Day Was Yesterday."

Hooyah.

GPS

Orienteering is the skill of navigating over land and forest with a compass and a terrain map…

Waypoints are marked on trees and all you have is a compass and map to help you try to find it.

Really fun if getting somewhere matters.

We used our underwater compass to direct us towards ships at night. Dark harbors, oxygen rebreathers, no bubbles. Have to come up several times to make sure your course was good. Then you had to commit and swim until you felt the hull. Spooky if you didn't love it.

Finding your way. Today? Well it is GPS all the way. Everyone knows exactly where they are all the way. Destinations can be marked and viewed via satellite.

The kids say today in amazement "You used a compass? What is that??" Duuhh, I don't know…

Some destinations are really important to find. Targets, especially when evil, exist. Even Amazon is talking about delivering pizza via GPS drones. Go figure?

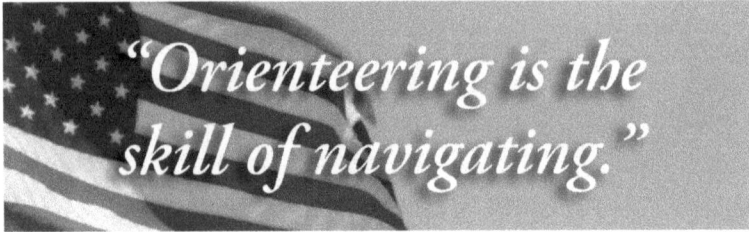

> ## "Orienteering is the skill of navigating."

We have all the answers. And they are all digital.

Moral certitude. Now that is a complicated destination. Most don't care to know that it could even be on one's map. But if nobody gets there, then society will cease to exist. Huuuhh?

There are courses to take and ones to avoid. Our problem is we want "easy" and we want "feel-good". We want to make sure we are happy and are not cheated out of pleasures that others get to enjoy. So our compass just spins as it is caught by false magnets. Dizzy confusion. Where is true north? Where is True?

True can be found on the road to Faith. It is uphill. The road is filled with sweat and doubt. No compass is needed. No GPS is needed. Our heart tells us what is right and wrong.

Why don't we follow it?

Who makes this compass?

In Heaven?

Hooyah.

Get the Tan

I don't know for sure when it all started.

But sometime as a kid I met this UDT guy and he had this tan.

He also had this neck chain with something on it.

I heard they had some joint in St. Thomas called the Silver Bullet... where frogs and stewardesses congregated and did the meringue ….. Tans were mandatory.

What is it about a tan? Girls sure look great in them.

Then there are the cruise ships of today. How do you walk the deck without tripping over a lounge chair? Why do hotels ruin the natural beauty with rows and rows of closely packed beach tanners? In Italy they have it down to a science. Good luck getting into the water.

I think the SEALs of today are so busy training and travelling that it is hard to find the few days to get The Tan. To them it is now a real luxury.

Who ever heard of a tan on a submarine? And the SEALs are the only ones to get topside ever so briefly before back in the water anyway….

A tan used to be a pseudo status symbol. Men who sailed and had yachts had them.

But…. you can't judge a man by the color of his skin.

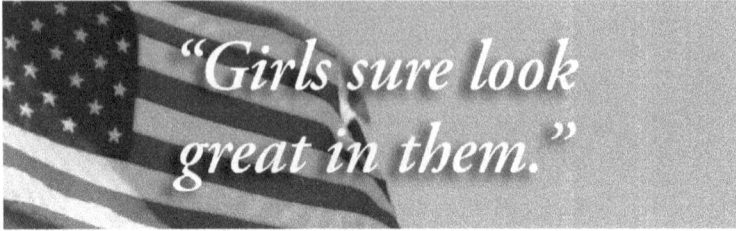

"Girls sure look great in them."

Our greatest sin is judging others, looking for easy ways to form an intelligent appraisal from afar. Color is often the first filter. It is usually downhill from there.

How can you judge the substance of a man without knowing his heart?

And without knowing His heart?

Life can bring you humility and wisdom only if you discard ego and pride.

Only if you learn that helping others is the first act that defines one.

And helping not just your peers but anyone, even the dirty.

Yes, you can and should judge and attack evil.

But learning how to judge takes wisdom, commitment, and integrity.

You will make mistakes.

You will be chastised.

Too bad.

We have to learn the Way.

Hooyah.

Drown It Out

Ever gone swimming way out far?

Like so far that you can't see land?

For 8-9 hours?

It gets creepy as you don't know where you might drown. And nobody will ever find you. Other than some big grey fish with lots of teeth.

Now if you have fins, a mask, compass, and a swim buddy you have things to look at while passing the time. Lots of it. Kick, stroke, and glide ad nauseam.

But by never quitting you get somewhere…

They didn't have waterproof ear buds back then. Of course if they did then you wouldn't hear your buddy drowning or getting eaten.

I think there is a growing problem these days.

The "ear-budders" have no clue what is going on around them. Hell, ISIS could shoot 20 people while they have "Happy" turned way up.

I think there is a message here.

I see people walking, running, and working out on machines and

"Ever gone swimming way out far?"

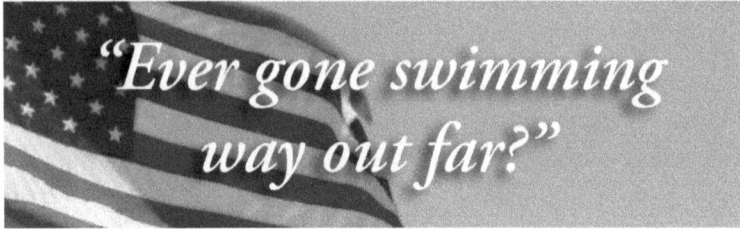

treadmills totally absorbed in the "me" of music. It helps detach one from the discomfort and effort of exercise.

Symbolic of the seduction of all social networking? Artificial protection from reality if overused and abused?

Silence is deadly. That is if the outside world is silent to you. Your aural reverie sets you up for trouble........

Of course, as with anything, moderation is a key to control and reasonable results. But who entertains moderation if pleasure or relief from discomfort is available? And it is if the ear buds are turned up..... Bee Gees? Maroon 5? ... Anyone?

You never know what they are listening to..... They are drowning out reality.

It is like we are becoming experts at making reality go away.

The most unreal TV shows are the reality shows!!! They contribute to the confusion of what is reality. Who defines reality?

Drown it out...! Drown it out...! Drown it out....! chant the worldwide billions of "ear-budders".

What is going to happen to the drowned when evil approaches and starts taking them one by one?

Drown it out with drinking, drown it out with uninformed thinking.

I am keeping my mask and fins at my side.

You ain't taking me down.

Hooyah.

WAG

Dogs wag their tails.

There is no guesswork figuring out why.

It usually means they are happy or anticipating/begging being fed.

Or best of all, you just walked into the room.

Nothing better than a dog.

I had this mixed Black Lab that went everywhere with me. Jumped off the boat if I did. Ran 4 miles in the dark at 5 AM with me. Went orienteering with SEAL candidates…. Could leave him outside on a run line all day… Slept near me. Warned better than any alarm. His name was Curtis. I miss him… I made this green neon sign for my office that says "Curtis Lives".

His wag was the start of all our waggers since. Puppy love.

But we are talking about the other WAG that is often as important. For sometimes critical decisions have to be made on the run… instantly. We call it, laughingly, the Wild-Ass-Guess. You have to be good at them or you will be dead.

It pays to train and train and train so you reduce the WAG factor to a

"Dogs wag their tails."

minimum. Yet, in the face of peril, someone has to offer the WAG for all to consider and act upon.

The sniper manages his breath, measures all the variables, but then the real menace of the human target often becomes a WAG.... And he "sends it".

It is important to assess all our WAGs so we are learning from them and reducing them.

I contend that a thorough involvement with the Bible is essential.

Find a version that works for you. If it is confusing don't quit. Find a church or person who can interpret and make it enjoyable. Don't get caught up in the memorizing folly. It is the Spirit that is to be sought out.

It is harder and better than being a SEAL.

This is not a WAG.

Hooyah.

Sight Unseen

The greatest works of man have not been seen.

The mother alone at night holding her child until exhausted.

The policeman holding a terrified victim.

Thanking a waitress.

None seen, but as important as all the seen.

Most like not to be seen when they do good.

It's a pride thing.

Then we have all the damned evil in the world that goes unseen.

And the evil we choose not to see.

The abuse of woman and child remains not attacked.   No priority.
That is evil squared.

Who do we have to help us? Prayer is essential to prioritize, to clear the mind for decision.

Who to send?

I know who we send and they like to be unrecognized. They choose to

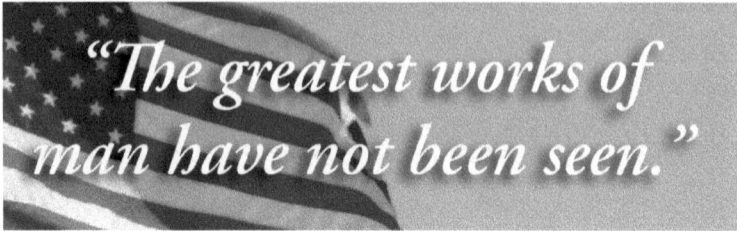

"The greatest works of man have not been seen."

be unseen. In fact their only safety comes from not being seen. Sight unseen. We must let them have it back and have media grow up and look the other way.

I have no problem with using stealth to shoot evil in the back.

We have to get over our need to give evil a second chance.

Not to doubt our own ability to assess and judge.

Evil must die sight unseen.

Hooyah.

VVV

HHH is a professional wrestler.

BBB is the Better Business Bureau.

AAA helps you with your cars.

Triple X was a movie with Vin Diesel and is a symbol of evil.

Triple Crown is the ultimate in horse racing.

Brand new is Triple V, VVV, Veterans Visiting Veterans. An idea I hatched for my Vets in church to be more active.

We established a relationship with an assisted living facility and met with Veterans there. My concept is for each one of us to meet once a week, for one hour only, with the same veteran. Each having their own different individual. Just for conversation and companionship, nothing religious.

You well know that we Veterans have our own language and are rather private about our experience.

There are veteran's associations out there, but none come close to this....

But when away from beer and alcohol in a private setting the sharing can be phenomenal.

"Triple your pleasure..."

When coaxed and assured that you are sincere, the stories flow from WWII to Korea to Vietnam to the present. Whether a clerk or a pilot, all served their country with pride. How they enlisted is a blast and humbling.

Telling the truth to fellow comrades is like a breath of fresh air. The humor is still there. Special.

A new friend, old Steve, has taken ownership of this ministry for me. His time in the service in Vietnam was rough. Hard to forget. But he has risen above the pain.

All who served are privately proud but quiet. Only 5% enlist today, the rest have no clue.

Our veterans all believe in a universal draft too.

VVV. Veterans Visiting Veterans.

Triple your pleasure......

Kinda cool? Eh??

Hooyah.

Eulogy

When it comes time for the eulogy… who is going to say what?

I wonder if that person is going to say the right thing.

I hope they don't ask that other person to say something.

Will my wife be crying?

Will my daughters say the right thing?

Sure glad I will be busy elsewhere.

Spare me the video.

I hope it will be in a real church with real pews, not on the beach and ocean which I loved a lot too… After my stents and bypass surgery I got to live well beyond my Dad's years…if this is an accomplishment. Did the world benefit??? Or at least my world??? Or was I just a consumer? Of time…?

I have heard others' eulogies and they left me kind of cold (pun intended). They talked about the love of family, vacations enjoyed, hobbies and sports. Business career and other accomplishments… even generosities… and "he loved this and that" ad nauseam. For the most part they sound a lot alike.

"Will my wife be crying?"

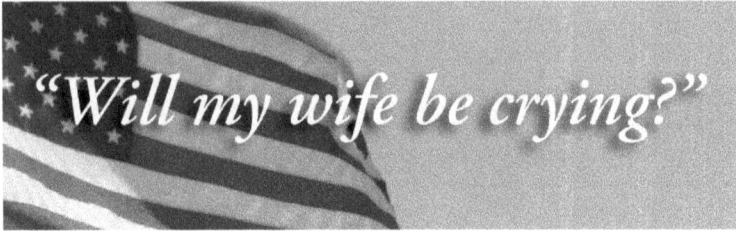

The pursuit of titles, money, or recognition traps so many on a street to nowhere. At eulogies you hear litanies of the material and passing allusions to compassion. Religion??? Gotta be careful...

What were you meant to be?... rings in my ears... did you achieve it? Did you figure out what life is all about and make sure you fulfilled your promise?

Somehow I feel that journeys end too soon. Life just can't be about the last years of golf... or finding a good church, and watching your pennies. Who were you meant to be? Or who could you have been???

Did you stand up for what is right? Did you define good and fight evil?

I have an intriguing résumé: Yale, Navy SEALs (UDT), great daughters, great travels, finishing with my wife's incredible business story. Who would have believed???

Yet all this would be meaningless if someone did not mention Jesus and my extraordinary involvement with Him. Only the few know I was His rogue apostle chosen to lead others out of the walls that kept them from being splendid spiritual butterflies.

That is the story worth telling.

Joys to share with others that transcends all other relationships.

Boy, was I blessed to have the perseverance to not quit on God.

If I were alive during my eulogy I would shout out loud, "Don't quit on Jesus!"…

What you can't yet see is just around the corner if you keep moving forward.

Godspeed & love,

Dad

Hooyah.

One World

Celebrities gather and sing "We Are The World"….

Do we?

From space our diversities are irrelevant…

We celebrate our differences and our cultures.

But at birth we do look so alike.

We are family.

When a woman or child is abused anywhere it is really to your family.

Except we can't see it that way.

We desecrate God with intellectual dismissal.

But without Him, there is no family. There is no Father.

The SEALs are some of those who are on the very dangerous front lines of confronting this evil indifference.

To do nothing is like leaving your front door open with your children inside, alone.

There are evil forces out there in nations and religions that wish us harm.

"Brave men are needed more than ever."

Our heads are in the sand to the cloaked threats of annihilation.

Brave men are needed more than ever.

One world is the noble dream.

"We are the world".

Hooyah.

EPILOGUE

I have been blessed with a journey that has not seen the real poverty or felt the real pain of the majority. Please don't judge me by the immaterial, much less the material. I was born in Bronxville, NY in 1940. Grew up in Louisville and St Louis. Graduated from Yale and went into the Navy. I had the great honor of fulfilling my dream to become a Frogman. I graduated from BUDS Class 31E, Basic Underwater Demolition/Seal School. I was an officer in Underwater Demolition Team 21 which became Seal Team 4 in 1984. I had the honor of recovering several spacecraft, including Gemini 6/7 & AS-201, the very first Apollo Spacecraft to go into space. Wow, did I luck out. Then I spent 40 years in women's retail, in various department stores. Even a year at the World Wrestling Federation... go figure?

I have two great daughters and two grandchildren who have just discovered the water and facemasks. My wife has created probably the #1 women's accessory store in the country as evidenced by how much she is copied. Therein I work and report to her... No comment. LOL.

As you can tell by reading between the lines there is a spiritual side to my journey. Kind of covert as I just want to make a difference unseen.

God Bless You All... Happy Trails.

ACKNOWLEDGEMENTS

Writing 1-800-FOR-SEALS-ONLY was never planned. My experiences were minor compared to the SEALs of today... but they serve as a backdrop for trying to communicate what is most important in life. And that is what you value. I do not preach. I only try to provoke you to think while laughing. Aka multi-tasking.

The chapters average only 300 words. There is no planned order. You can open the book anywhere and read the 2 pages and get a smile and a frown if you catch the serious challenge.

Maybe these books will be found some day and help others make fewer mistakes.

I have to always acknowledge those who make a difference to me. This is the short list.

My winter of 64 BUD/S (UDTR) 31E Classmates are Baldwin, Brantly, Crosby, Dasilva, Detmer, Feltman, Fletcher, Fraser, Guhareff, Gormly, Kennedy, McCarthy, Robinson, Rodger, Schropp, Serra, Sobrinho, Spillane, Sweesy, Tomsho, Trinidade, Woolf, Ziegler.....

And then over the years other Naval Special Warfare friends... Janke, Jones, Truxell, Jerussi, Shea, Blais, Sutherland, Heinlein, Hawes, Hawkins, Bisset, Black, Diviney, Riojas, LeMoyne, Lyons

I cannot leave out special clergy... Alarcon, DeMarco, Merry, Merriam,

Sauter, Brown, Wood, Leininger, Wicker, Hinson, and others along the way who planted the seeds I needed.

And who started it all, Ruth & Bud, my parents, for gifts I am still counting. And... for my little brother, Dennis, who reminded me when I was wrong.

Then there are my daughters, Candice and Courtney, who thought they knew their dad, but really didn't. There is my brilliant wife Christina, who thought she knew her husband..... And then there are my friends from the past whose life journeys I do not fully know, and who do not know me now. For in life it is who we become, not who we were.

So many people inhabit the fabric of our lives. So many played unseen roles in the writing of my six books. 1-800-I-AM-UNHAPPY Vol. 1 & Vol. 2 are good, 1-800-FOR WOMEN-ONLY is fabulous, and 1-800-LAUGHING-OUT-LOUD is great and fun…. The 5th is 1-800-OH-MY-GOODNESS. And now, this the 6th you have read... 1-800-FOR-SEALS-ONLY… except that it is for everybody.

Lastly, there are Sandra Simmons-Dawson and Brian Dawson who helped edit and format the books, website, and marketing. Their firm, Money Management Solutions, Inc. dba Customer Finder Marketing http://customerfindermarketing.com/ is a gem.

www.ingramcontent.com/pod-product-compliance
Lightning Source LLC
Chambersburg PA
CBHW071523040426

42452CB00008B/860